A HEALTHIER HAPPIER YOU

101 Steps for Lessening Stress

LORRAINE BOSSÉ-SMITH

BARBOUR
PUBLISHING

Published by Barbour Publishing, Inc., P.O. Box 719,
Uhrichsville, Ohio 44683, www.barbourbooks.com

*Our mission is to publish and distribute inspirational products
offering exceptional value and biblical encouragement to the
masses.*

 Member of the
Evangelical Christian
Publishers Association

Printed in the United States of America.
5 4 3 2 1

DEDICATION

To my parents,
James and Mildred (Millie) Bossé,
who died much too young.
Thank you for giving all you had,
loving me, and encouraging me to
"be better than the best."
I think you'd be proud of
the woman I have become.
I will always love and miss you.

CONTENTS

ACKNOWLEDGMENTS

I want to thank Shannon Hill, a peer and friend, for the opportunity to write this book. I appreciate your willingness to put your belief in me into action. Because of you, I can improve the quality of people's lives through this book. Thank you for also being a friend who isn't afraid to be real and authentic. You are one in a million, girl!

To Nancy Jernigan, my agent, I want to thank you for all your hard work in representing me through the process and allowing me to focus my energies on writing. I greatly appreciate our rekindled friendship and know God brought us together for this purpose.

To Marion Terrell, who is a cheerleader and inspiration, thank you for reviewing my manuscript and providing loving feedback. You are one special lady and a living example of how managing one's stress better can overcome health issues, no matter what the doctors say.

To my many friends, thank you for loving me, encouraging me and praying for me during this process. You are all one of the best stress busters I know!

To my husband, Steve, thank you for loving me. Without you, I may not have had the confidence to spread my wings and fly.

Success Contract

I, _____, hereby make a commitment
to read this book with the intent
of changing my thoughts and approach
towards living a healthy lifestyle.

I agree to try at least 30 of the suggested tips
on how to reduce and manage stress
for a period of at least 30 days.

When I have kept this agreement, I give myself
permission to celebrate by

Signature: _____

Date: _____

Witness: _____

Date: _____

INTRODUCTION

STRESS. This small word is responsible for more illness and unhappiness than we can imagine. Whether we are starting a new job, buying our first home, having a baby, going through a divorce, dealing with a loved one's death, or simply existing, we are experiencing stress. We live with it every day.

I love the commercial from a few years ago that depicted a tormented young man at the grocery store checkout being asked "Paper or plastic?" Behind his blank stare, his mind whirls with options: "If I get the paper, how many trees had to die? But, if I get the plastic, will it overflow landfills?"

Meanwhile the clerk is still asking, "Paper or plastic?" The fifteen people lined up behind him are impatient and frustrated, but he just can't decide. He's overloaded and stressed out! We laugh at the commercial because it is too close to home. We are all stressed out, and usually the smallest of details—such as paper or plastic—pushes us over the edge.

So, what exactly *is* stress?

According to Dr. Hans Seyle, founder of Stress Management Research, "Stress is the wear and tear on your body caused by life's events."

Stress is the body's physical and chemical reactions to circumstances that frighten, excite, confuse,

anger, endanger, and irritate us. Think about it:
Ulcers, headaches, muscle tension, and the common
cold can all result from stress. Stress affects each of
us. It is no wonder we are stressed as we live in a fast-
food society and have the treadmill on warp speed. It
seems to be the American way: Work more, make
more, spend more, and then work even harder to
make even more money so you can buy even more
stuff! The result for us is more stress, and it is costly:

- One million Americans have a heart
  attack each year.
- Thirteen billion doses of tranquilizers,
  barbiturates, and amphetamines are
  prescribed yearly.
- Eight million Americans have stomach ulcers.
- Fifty thousand stress-related suicides
  each year (only 1 in 8 is successful).
- Twelve million plus alcoholics in this
  country alone.

*A brave person may not live forever,
but someone who lives in fear never really lives.*

ANONYMOUS

Stress-related illness continues to rise. The National

Mental Health Association reports that 75 percent to 95 percent of *all* visits to physicians are stress related. Poor health equals poor quality of life for you and for me, and that isn't how God intended for us to live.

In 1997, I realized I no longer wanted to work eighty hours a week under high amounts of stress for my employer. So, I decided to create my own business as a consultant. I wanted to use my God-given gifts to help businesses with marketing, leadership, and sales consulting. With prayer and trembling, I launched LB & Associates. As time passed and circumstances changed, I expanded my services to include professional coaching and corporate training. I married Steve, whose company was called Concept One, Inc., and we began operating as a team. No matter what the project, I began to get more and more involved with people on a personal level. I always understood the concept that we are complex beings and can't isolate certain aspects of our makeup, however, I was concerned about being able to address this in professional settings and make a decent living. I learned that people are desperately seeking balance at home and at work.

If we are under duress at work, it comes home and can ruin marriages. If we are unhealthy physically or mentally, this follows us to the office and can cause us to lose our jobs. What is stress costing you: Money? Work? Family? Friends? Illness? Peace? Sleep? Joy? Love? Life?

I have always loved living a healthy, active lifestyle. I finally entered the fitness industry several years ago. I received certifications enabling me to focus on the "total person." I now train people to reach their fitness goals, while working with the entire person. The professional term is "wellness," which includes balancing our emotional, mental, physical, and spiritual aspects of life. So often, we are good at addressing one or two segments of life, but the other portions suffer. Without balance, stress can take its toll on us, not only reducing the *quality* of our life, but often decreasing its *quantity*.

God gives life to each of us. We usually start off on the right path, but circumstances derail us and *BAM!* Stress kicks in. We can't always change our circumstances, but we *can* manage our responses better. Although stress *is* a fact of life on earth, how we deal with stress is up to us! I want to help you beat stress.

Both a hero and a coward feel fear.
The difference is that the
hero doesn't allow fear to dictate his behavior.

ANONYMOUS

Every day we face decisions. We choose what clothes to wear, which roads to drive on, what food to eat, what we will do with our free time, and how we will spend our money. Every time we make a decision to do one thing, we are choosing to *not* do everything else. This is called "opportunity cost." Everything has an opportunity cost, but we must decide if we are willing to pay the price. Some choices are easy, such as the decision to play with your child or fold clothes that can wait until tomorrow. Others are more difficult and require thought, consideration, and prayer. No one can make these decisions for you. But, thankfully, we have God to guide and direct us.

The following pages are designed to help you manage all aspects of your life better. The tips, suggestions, and ideas will help you regroup your emotions, refocus your mind, reenergize your body, and reconnect with your Maker. In other words, they'll enable you to live a healthier life!

Regroup your emotions
Refocus your mind
Reenergize your body
Reconnect with your Maker

TO LIVE a healthier life, you must first want to change for the better. Secondly, you must commit to do whatever is necessary to improve your life. This is easy to say, but hard to do. I encourage you to uncover your motivation for making this change, and it will help you keep your commitment. For example, a working mother may be spending too much time at the office and, therefore, isn't as patient with her children at home as she would like to be. She is too tired to help with homework or to play with her youngsters. Her kids feel unloved and begin getting into trouble. Her motivation might be to set boundaries at work in order to reduce stress so that she can provide a loving, nurturing environment for her children at home.

What's your motivation? Why reduce stress and live a healthier life?

As you read this book, I suggest you reflect on

your current state and ask yourself these questions:

- Where is your stress coming from?
- What is it costing you (emotionally, physically, spiritually, professionally)?
- What do you have control over and what can you change?
- What would your life look like if things were different?
- How would you feel and what positive things would result from less stress?

Please know that I am rooting for you! Hopefully you know that you deserve a healthier life. . . one free of stress and chaos! May the following pages help you discover a better way, believe in yourself to make the necessary changes, and find the courage to beat stress!

Life is a fragile gift from God. Between this book, prayer, and your efforts, I hope you will discover a new life for yourself. . .one that is new and improved! Let's enjoy the journey and live a more balanced, healthier life!

SECTION I

REGROUPING OUR EMOTIONS

1
Live a Little and Have Fun!

REMEMBER being a carefree child running barefoot in the grass chasing butterflies? We didn't have much stress back then. No wonder we fondly recollect "the good old days." I believe, however, that we can and should have fun as adults. All work and no fun can make us very grumpy!

Being a grown-up certainly is work, and it isn't always fun. We have responsibilities to many programs and a variety of people, but we must not forget that one of our most important responsibilities is to ourselves. We cannot do anything or be anything for anyone else if we do not first take care of ourselves and our emotional needs.

What makes you laugh? What gives you joy? What energizes you and melts the stress? Each of us is uniquely made, so chances are, our favorite things are different. Whether it's doing a crossword puzzle, eating an ice-cream sundae, going for a run, or buying a new pair of shoes, make sure you live a little every once in awhile and have fun! You will feel better, and you will have much more to give as a result.

Live as you will wish to have lived
when you are dying.

CHRISTIAN FURCHTEGOTT GELLERT

2
Give and Receive Love

LOVE. It's such a small word, but more songs, more poems, more movies, and more books have been on the topic of love than any other subject. Love has the power to ignite our dormant power, allowing us to accomplish amazing feats. Love inspires people to be better and do more with their lives, and it is why men can face the horrors of war with courage. We need love to live a healthy life. Give it freely and often! God *is* love and created us to also *be* loved. Are you letting Him and others love you?

We typically have no problem giving love to others; this is especially true for women. By women's design and nature, we are caretakers, giving of ourselves to others. In fact, we tend to put other people's needs before our own. What we fail to do, however, is let ourselves *be* loved.

I used to struggle with receiving gifts of love until I heard a message preached on the subject. I don't remember who spoke or where I was, but the message stuck with me. Love cannot be given unless it is first received. In Acts 20:35 Jesus said, "It is more blessed to give than to receive." If I refuse someone's gift of love, I have just denied that person the joy of giving. As a result, I prevent both of us from being blessed. Do I really want to interfere with what someone else feels he or she wants to do? No, I do not!

The world needs love. You and I need love. We would all benefit from giving a little more love and offering less judgment and criticism. Just remember that someone also wants to give love to you. Let them—and let love come into your life!

❧

Love is to the heart
what the summer is to the farmer's year.
It brings to harvest
all the loveliest flowers of the soul.

BILLY GRAHAM

3

Set Your Perimeter and Honor It

IN A DAY when we expect "free roaming" for our cell phones and don't want to be fenced into a contract, we may have difficulty understanding the concept of boundaries. But, as long as land has existed, we have created lines that define "what is mine" and "what is yours" and "what is theirs." Ask any farmer or cattle rancher and they know exactly where their property begins and ends. They have probably fenced their perimeter to help others clearly see the dividing line.

Our lives are no different, no matter if we live in a small apartment or on acreage.

Do you know anyone who has had a nervous breakdown? Chances are that they gave too much and never set limits. Then one day, they had nothing left to give and collapsed.

Think of your emotions like a bank account. If you only make withdrawals, your account becomes overdrawn or empty. People in church leadership often fall into this trap and burn out completely. We all must protect ourselves by understanding what we *can* give, what we are *willing* to give, and what we are *able* to give. By defining our perimeter, we are protecting "our land" from unwanted vandals and thieves. Sometimes, we are simply setting "visiting hours" so that we can ensure we are ready and able to give. And since we give to so many people, it is important for us to set boundaries with all relationships: co-workers, bosses, spouses, kids, family members, and friends. Although we may be good at setting limits at home, we may not be as diligent at the office (or vice versa). Practice protecting your emotional bank account so you don't become overdrawn.

Then, when you set those limits, make sure you honor them. In doing so, you will reduce your stress and care for your mental, emotional, and physical states. You are the only "you" on this planet. Be good to yourself.

Sometimes it is more important to
discover what one cannot do,
than what one can do.

LIN YUTANG

4
Live Within Your Budget

FINANCIAL issues are one of the major causes of divorces today in America. Money *does* matter. We need it to live. Unfortunately, pursuing it often leaves us empty, drained, and lifeless.

Many people don't like the word "budget" because it feels restrictive, just like the word "diet." However, neither of these words alone is really negative. In fact, each is positive. Our "diet" is what we eat, and our "budget" is what we live within. Our diet includes eating what we need to survive. Our budget should be the same way: Budget what you need to live.

One of the biggest mistakes people make in creating their budgets is being unrealistic. In order to make their budget numbers look smaller on paper, they arbitrarily change amounts they plan to spend. But that number shifting on paper is not always practical. For example, if your weekly grocery bill is $100, why would you budget $50? You probably will not suddenly eat less and save $50. No, you need $100, so budget it. If you know you're going to rent a movie every weekend, list it and budget for it. Don't just hope you won't spend the money when you know you will. Be honest with yourself. The more accurately your budget reflects your life, the better control you can take.

That's the second and more difficult part. Once you have established your budget, you can begin to compare it to income, manage it, and adjust it. We all have areas we can reduce and improve. Look for those areas where you can cut back so your budget can work within your income—unless you are in sales or another field in which you can increase your income to match your spending.

The bottom line is that to reduce stress, we must live within our means. When we step outside of those boundaries, we create worry and anxiety, not to mention financial strain and possible disaster. Money is not evil, but horrible things can happen if we don't manage it well. Make money work for you, not the other way around.

The best things in life are free.

ANONYMOUS

5
Laugh

I love to laugh, loud and long and clear.

MARY POPPINS
Disney Movie

I THANK God for the range of emotions He has given us. Life never has a dull moment, and we can react, respond, and feel an array of emotions to match any situation. But not all emotions are positive. Stress can suck energy out of us and wreak havoc on our emotions. When faced with the lion's den, laugh.

Laughing is so good for us. Have you ever tried to be stressed out, angry, or sad when you were laughing? It's hard to do. Having a bad day? Laugh! Feeling overwhelmed? Laugh out loud! Weary? Roll on the floor and laugh. Besides making yourself feel better, remember the old saying from *Solitude, Stanza I*, "When you laugh, the world laughs with you. . . ."

*Of all the things God created,
I am often most grateful He created laughter.*

CHARLES SWINDOLL

6
Think the Best of Others

I REMEMBER learning about the "self-fulfilling prophecy" in school. The gist was that whatever you expected, you would get. What a powerful concept! Not only does it impact our life, but it also influences our relationships with others.

When we think negative things about another person ("She hurt my feelings on purpose"), we not only determine our behavior toward that person, but we also influence how he or she will interact with us. That person will sense our negativity and basically deliver what we have asked for. . .ouch!

*Treat people as if they were what they should be,
and you help them become what
they are capable of becoming.*

JOHANN WOLFGANG VON GOETHE

Do you want stronger, healthier relationships? Want less stress? Then decide this very moment to think the best of others! Expect their best, and you just might get it.

We awaken in others
the same attitude of
mind we hold toward them.

ELBERT HUBBARD

7
Journal

I HAVE written in journals during most of my life. I
have found it quite comforting to confide in their
pages my hopes, dreams, hurts, disappointments, frustrations, and a myriad of other emotions. Emotions
are strange. Until we let ourselves fully experience
them, the thoughts triggering them will not let go. If
you are upset about something yet you never express
it, it will stick with you, burn inside of you, and eventually it may run you down. I believe much of the
stress we carry is unresolved emotions. Let it go! And
a good outlet for this is writing it in a journal.

If you are not used to writing, do not be intimi-
dated. Journaling isn't just for the poetic and gifted.
In fact, one reason I enjoy it so much is because I
know no one else will ever see the words and thoughts
I scribble, sometimes almost illegibly because of my
intense feelings at the moment. Journaling is private,
and a journal can become your best friend. Writing
down your feelings is also a great way to give your
worries and cares to the Lord.

Cast your cares on the LORD, and he will sustain you.

PSALM 55:22

I encourage you to try journaling for a month. You don't have to write every day, but you may find it very healing to address each day's emotions as you feel them. Write out what is going on, what you think, how you feel, and then close the book. As you express your emotions, their ability to control you loses power. You are then free to live with less stress and more energy.

I recently took my journals from several years to the beach, where a girlfriend and I had a "journal burning party." These particular journals represented very painful times in each of our lives. These journals were our saving grace during those times, but it was now time for us to move forward. We needed to rid ourselves of the negative associations these journals had and be free. So, we burned them! Up in a cloud of smoke went anger, frustration, disappointments, sadness, devastation, and resentment. Our former pain floated away in the wind. We each had some parting words and then ran into the water, celebrating new days ahead. It was invigorating and uplifting!

Words have power. Release them into the confidential pages of a journal.

❧

Until you make peace with who you are,
you will never be content with what you have.

Doris Mortman

8
Share with a Friend

I STILL recall my friends' shock when I announced my divorce back in 1996. "We thought you were happy," they said. I was in a physically and mentally abusive relationship that just about destroyed me, but they didn't know because I didn't tell them. One friend was angry with me and said, "How can I be your friend and pray for you if I don't know what is going on?"

She was right. We aren't designed to handle the burden of stress alone; God gives us friends.

The weight of decisions or struggles is much heavier when we choose to carry the load without help. Rather than keeping everything inside and always putting on your happy face, spend time with a friend. I make it a point to have lunch with key friends every once in awhile so we cannot only update one another about our lives, but we can share heart to heart.

I will say this: Choose your friends wisely. Not everyone is mature enough to keep your challenges confidential. The last thing you want is your entire neighborhood hearing about the fight you and your spouse had. Take care to select a friend who is healthy, mature, and spiritual. And don't look to your friends to be just a dumping ground. Sharing should go both ways so that you may each care for one another, support each other, and pray for healing. Thank God for friends!

I am blessed to have friends all around the country. Each friend is unique, and we connect on different levels based on our common interests. Have friends who can meet an array of needs. To expect one person to be everything may be expecting too much. But, who couldn't use more friends anyway?

By listening, by caring,
by playing you back to yourself,
friends ratify your better instincts
and endorse your unique worth.
Friends validate you.

GAIL SHEEHY

9
Cry

I REMEMBER when my family decided to leave the East Coast and move out west. We had a grand going-away party to send us on our way to new horizons in Colorado, and we bid farewell to a lifetime of friends and family. That evening, I saw my father cry for the first time in my eleven years of life. He was overwhelmed with sadness and uncertainty of the unknown. He was stressed, and he let it out. What a great lesson for all of us.

Crying is so very healing. I really don't quite understand it, but I do accept it. When the tears start flowing, emotions release. Toxins in our systems even seem to let go and move on. When was the last time you cried? I mean, had a really good cry?

We often think others expect us to be strong, so we fight against our desire to release tears. Please don't. Even Jesus wept. God created this wonderful experience so we can express ourselves and heal the hurts within. When we bottle up our feelings, they'll eventually come out one way or another. It's okay to cry now and then. It only means you are human.

I turned off that emotion for a long period in my life. My situation was too intense. I was afraid if

I cried I wouldn't be able to stop. Ever feel that way? I finally let go one night after meeting my now husband, Steve. I felt safe in his arms and released years of pent-up tears. Although I had puffy eyes when I was done, I felt my load had been lifted. I felt more at peace. Everything has a season—even weeping. Don't forget to cry when you need to and let the healing begin.

With each sunrise,

we start anew.

ANONYMOUS

10
Play

I LIKE TO work. No matter what job I have ahead of me, I am one of those rare individuals who enjoys tackling it. To me, being productive is a gift. All that said, though, I *love* to play! And I play hard.

Whether it is hiking, biking, playing tennis, running, competing in races, joining a game of volleyball, going on a picnic, or challenging my husband to a game of Scrabble, I have fun. I also let go of the day, its worries, and my stress. Playing is an outlet for all the negative garbage that can build up.

What do *you* do for fun?

I am amazed when I hear that someone has a bunch of vacation time they'll lose if they don't use it right away. Excuse me? I can't comprehend why anyone would not use his or her hard-earned time off. Even when I was working eighty hours a week, I took time off. Time off to play is paramount to our good health.

Even if you have to block off times to play and plan it, do so! Play a game with some friends or simply play with a child. Children are magnificent that way. They instantly give us perspective on what's *truly* important, and the rest of the world and its troubles seem to melt away. Recess isn't just for kids; we all need to play.

&

Sing to him a new song;
play skillfully, and shout for joy.

PSALM 33:3

11
Pick Wildflowers

THIS YEAR I experienced my first spring in southern California. I had never imagined such a glorious display of wildflowers. The colors were brilliant: orange, purple, yellow, and white. The hills were alive!

Maybe I'm a die-hard romantic, but when I thought of wildflowers, I pictured walking through rolling hills, knee-high in God's creation, without a care in the world. It was such a good vision, I thought I should try it and so I did.

Nature is beautiful and has so much to offer us. It is changing every second. Get outside, get some fresh air, and take a walk. Absorb some of the positive, healthy energy that growing things seem to emanate. Gather some of its beauty and take it home with you. Make a lovely floral arrangement as a memento of the day. And if you begin to feel a bit stressed, inhale the delightful scent and revisit the wildflower patch, if only in your imagination.

You are the only you the world has.
Take very good care of yourself!

12
Bake Cookies

WHEN WE were getting ready to sell our home, our real estate agent gave us some "showing tips." Apparently, if we put away the clutter, left warm lights on, and played soothing music, we would increase our chances of obtaining a buyer. Another suggestion: Bake cookies.

My mother-in-law tells the story of when they bought their first home. It was smaller than they wanted and not in a very good part of town, but the owner had just baked something fresh. The aroma overwhelmed them as they viewed the home, and they soon signed on the dotted line. Home *sweet* home was given a new meaning!

What images or feelings do you get when you smell freshly baked cookies? Most of us fondly recall our mother or grandmother baking us a special treat. Something magical happens when our noses whiff of something so tasty. We seem to relax.

Even if you don't have the time to make cookies from scratch, pick up a package or mix and bake some heartwarming, soul-soothing, stress-busting cookies. Savor the smell as they bake, and invite others to share them hot out of the oven with you. Then again, maybe not, if you are a "cookie monster."

ॐ

C is for cookie,
and that is good enough for me.

COOKIE MONSTER,
Sesame Street

13
Have a Pet

WHEN my mother passed away in 1997, I inherited her cat, Wuz. He is a full-bred Himalayan with powder blue eyes and a chocolate point face. My mom adored Wuz and spoiled him. He is like a little person and has become an important part of our family. Never did I imagine the impact that a small creature could have on me. He is one of my favorite stress reducers. He seems to always know when the pressure is on and strolls into my office at just the right time. He meows until I take notice, and then he rolls around and purrs. As I stroke his fluffy coat, I begin to take deeper breaths and gain perspective. All is well with the world.

Research shows that when animals are brought into nursing homes, patients' spirits improve. They tend to smile more and even laugh out loud at the site of these furry friends. Animals *are* healing, no doubt about it. I thank God that He created these little creatures for us to share life with.

Feeling a bit stressed? Cuddle up to your cat and let him rub against you and purr. Tense and uptight? Pet your dog and play catch. The love you receive will be unconditional and true. Animals don't care what kind of car you drive or what your credentials are. They simply want you.

Whatever your pet preference (dog, cat, bird, snake, bunny, fish, donkey, horse, reptile), bring one into your home. The love you give will be doubled in return.

♄

Sometimes, God's greatest gifts
come in small packages.

14
Watch Your Mouth

DID YOU ever hear those words while you were growing up? I remember that my mother was especially particular about the words I used. Once when I was in high school, I remember saying I was "p—off" in front of my mom. I got in trouble. It was "uncalled-for" language and rude. How far our society has come since then. Words once only permitted in R-rated movies are now heard in PG-13 movies as long as they don't occur too often. Such angry words create negative energy and stress. We need to watch what we say because it can, and usually will, dictate our mood.

The best advice I've heard about being angry is that your emotions should match the situation. In other words, if someone cuts you off in traffic, you may be inconvenienced, but are you really "ticked off" enough to explode? Try changing your words to truly match your circumstances. For example, "It irritates me when people cut me off" is much more reasonable. Also, avoid choosing negative words when speaking about others. No one wins when we use words that are judging or name calling. Words like "stupid," "jerk," and "moron" should be removed from our vocabulary, especially if we want to portray the light and draw people toward us.

If you are really up for a challenge, begin to select your words deliberately. Words can change your attitude and mood instantly. If you are feeling blue, tell yourself you are in a great mood. The more you say words like "I'm energetic, I'm creative, I'm happy, I'm full of joy," the more you will actually become what you say. On the flip side, if you state such things as "I'm depressed, I'm tired, I'm burned out," well then, you will reap what you sow. The word choice is yours: stress or health.

He who guards his lips guards his life,
but he who speaks rashly will come to ruin.

PROVERBS 13:3

15
Dream

ALTHOUGH I'm goal-oriented, I do like to window-shop. I enjoy the process of envisioning certain items in my home or pretending I could buy special gifts for people if money were no object. I really love clothes shopping because it doesn't cost anything to try on outfits. I'll have hours of entertainment and walk away without spending a penny. It is soothing and fun to dream for awhile.

Do you dream?

Obviously the things I've mentioned are small dreams. The larger the dream, the more we have to look forward to. I firmly believe that when we stop dreaming, we stop living happily. People can get into trouble when they think every dream must become a goal. This is when we can create stress and frustration for ourselves. Some dreams are certainly obtainable and should be realized. Other dreams are, well, for dreaming and relaxing. . .for entertainment.

I don't have a very good singing voice. Oh sure, I get by at church, but I'm nothing to write home about. But I do have a dream of being on stage singing to thousands of fans with rockin' music. Am I going to take singing lessons? Am I going to quit my job and move to Hollywood? Absolutely not! I just get a smile out of the thought every once in awhile, and it can relax me. Why? Because it isn't real. Sometimes, real life is too intense, and we must retreat for just a moment. Certainly, we never want to make it a habit to totally avoid real life, but a visit to dreamland now and then is a good thing. So, what would you do if money were no object?

Since it doesn't cost a dime to dream,
you'll never shortchange yourself
when you stretch your imagination.

ROBERT SCHULLER

16
Party

I WAS NEVER into the wild party scene, even when I was young. I do, however, like having fun with friends. Getting together with friends is a great way to release tension and let go of the week's stresses. When we set a date and invite people over, we make a commitment that we must keep. We may feel too tired to host anything, but once we are with friends, we will never regret the little energy it took to pull off a fun evening. Our friends are worth it, and so are we.

Try a tea party for your friends, ladies. I did this in a new town so I could get acquainted with everyone. We all dressed up in beautiful spring dresses and brought our favorite tea setting. I made a variety of tasty teas and homemade scones (you can buy them, too). We sat, listened to classical music, talked, and laughed the afternoon away. We got in touch with our feminine side and really bonded. It was a great party!

Guys, what about a Monday night football party where everyone brings a snack or drink, and you order pizza in? Start before the game so you have time to get acquainted. Throughout the evening, you'll enjoy talking about the statistics, plays, and referee calls.

You'll enjoy hanging out together and may even forget about your worries for just awhile.

You don't even have to call it a party, but I suggest you gather with some friends (old or new) and have some fun!

Happiness depends upon ourselves.

ARISTOTLE

17
Rent a Good Movie

I NEVER used to be able to sit still long enough to watch movies, but now that I am more relaxed, I have become a movie-aholic. I enjoy watching funny comedies and romantic love stories. Besides getting lost in the story for awhile, I appreciate the feelings and emotions a movie stirs up. Whether I'm laughing or crying, I easily find myself in the thick of the movie, experiencing the story right on my couch. It is hard to be stressed when you are someplace else!

I can see some movies countless times because I enjoy them so much. If you haven't seen one of my favorites, I could probably recite almost the entire movie for you. So go rent a movie, make some popcorn, cuddle under a blanket, and enjoy a good flick. Relax, let the mind go, and don't be afraid to express your feelings.

This is the day the LORD has made;
let us rejoice and be glad in it.

PSALM 118:24

18
Listen

I'M A praying woman. I talk to God all the time. He's my best friend. I learned some years ago, however, that I couldn't hear God. I prayed more and questioned why. It then hit me one day: I wasn't listening. In order to listen and *hear* God, I needed to be quiet! How could He speak to me if I never gave Him a chance? Is that happening with you?

Listening is certainly a skill that many people struggle with. Depending upon our family backgrounds, we may have been taught to wait our turn to speak, but our minds weren't listening. Instead, we were preparing our words.

Our minds race and never seem to stop, but we can halt them if we want to. Listen. I mean, really listen. Hear the words, see the expressions, watch the body language, and feel the emotions of the person talking. The more you work at listening to others (and God), the quieter your mind will be and the calmer your emotions will be. Shhhh. Be still and listen.

My dear brothers, take note of this:
Everyone should be quick to listen,
slow to speak and
slow to become angry.

JAMES 1:19

19
Seek Help

As a life coach, I help people along on their journeys. Whether they are pursuing a professional or personal goal, I offer strategies and solutions that result in success. I also listen and care for my clients' well-being. We all need that kind of assistance from time to time. In fact, I encourage each of you to have mentors—someone who is living as you would like to and is willing to share how he or she got there. Following a biblical example, each of us should have a Timothy (someone younger whom we can encourage), a Paul (a peer or equal to relate with), and a Barnabus (someone older and wiser to counsel and guide us).

Who do you have in your life to help manage your emotions and stress?

Sometimes it is difficult to find just the right person, but options to consider are: counselors, therapists, pastors, and life coaches. These people are trained to listen and support you as you work toward your objective. If they are really good, they won't do the work for you, but will guide you down the right path. They will stand beside you, cheer for you, care for you, and celebrate with you when you have met your goal. Let someone else help carry the burden.

We were not created to walk alone. Don't be afraid to seek help.

*People seldom improve when
they have no other model
but themselves to copy.*

OLIVER GOLDSMITH

20
Be Creative

I USED to love coloring when I was a child. Do you remember how proud you felt when your drawing was posted on the refrigerator? You were giving a piece of yourself to someone, and they accepted it. As adults, it is harder for us to find outlets for our creativity, but doing so is essential to our emotional health. If we shut out our creativity, we are shutting down positive energy and the ability to combat stress.

I like to explore ways to express myself and my creativity. Recently I discovered I have a flare for making floral arrangements. I have designed everything in our new home for a fraction of the cost I would pay to buy a finished creation from a store. I have even made some arrangements to be gifts. I assessed the person's home, color choices, and tastes. I would then wander through the hobby store and find just the right pieces and a vase to put them in. This has become an expression of my softer, creative side—something that I can give to others. What do you do?

Ever create a collage or dream board? What about painting or sculpting? How about cooking? Everyone has something that requires a creative touch. Don't be afraid to explore! Give a piece of yourself to the world, and you will be blessed.

Cherish your emotions
and never undervalue you.

ROBERT HENRI

21
Be a Good Neighbor

AS A CHILD, I was never a big fan of *Mr. Rogers' Neighborhood*; however, I did appreciate the wholesome principles he taught. As I grew and matured, I respected the man even more. He truly was a "good neighbor" to all. We lost a giving and kind man when he passed away.

Somehow, as a society, we need to get back to the basics and treat each other as we would like to be treated. We would certainly all have less stress if we did!

In earlier days, we used to see folks on a front porch drinking lemonade together and "fellowshipping." Too often today, we are in a rush and don't take the time to get to know our neighbors. We need to slow down and be neighborly.

On days when I'm working in my yard, I make sure that I don't have a tight schedule so I can take time to visit with neighbors. I'll even walk around to say "hi" and see what is new with their latest landscaping projects.

Building relationships isn't convenient. It takes time and effort. But when has the effort not paid off? Unless you are choosing the wrong people, you are always blessed by giving to a relationship.

Around holidays, I bake cupcakes or cookies for the kids in the neighborhood. It is a great excuse to visit with everyone. Take time to wave and smile as much as possible. Look out for your neighbor's house just as you would your own. You just might start a trend—and you might be amazed at how your neighborhood (and emotional well-being) changes for the better.

" 'Do not seek revenge or bear a grudge
against one of your people,
but love your neighbor as yourself.' "

LEVITICUS 19:18

22
Enjoy Some Hot Tea

MY MOTHER would be so proud of me now that I drink hot tea. For years, she tried every conceivable tactic to try to make me drink something warm since I was always cold. But, I would have nothing to do with hot drinks. Well, living a year in cold, damp Seattle cured me of that! Even though I moved to California five years ago, I now love drinking hot tea. Although it was a necessity in Washington, I now enjoy the finer traits of drinking hot tea. . .like relaxing and de-stressing.

We are fortunate these days to have a large assortment of herbal, decaffeinated teas that not only please our taste buds but also heal what ails us. I encourage you to have some on hand at all times and sip on a soothing cup when you feel those shoulders hiking up from tension.

Treasure today for we are not guaranteed a tomorrow.

Luxury need not have a price—
comfort itself is a luxury.

GEOFFREY BEENE

23
Act Responsibly

I DON'T know about you, but I've seen enough frivolous lawsuits. When people sue companies because their coffee is too hot, they are shifting blame to the wrong party to avoid their own failure or stupidity. Temporarily, these persons may feel better about the situation by shifting the blame; but in the long run, they will actually endure more emotional strain and hardship. Owning up to our own mistakes keeps our conscience clear and our emotions clean.

As children, most of us attempted to fake our parents out occasionally by saying, "I don't know how that got broken" or "I didn't do it." We are adults now, however, and it's time for us to grow up! Being responsible isn't always easy, but it is the right thing to do. Your soul (and God) knows when you do not take the high road. This division causes stress.

One way to ensure you are being responsible is to simply say what you mean and mean what you say. Double talk is for cowards. Remember what Grandma used to say: "If you don't have anything nice to say, don't say anything at all!" She was right. If living a life of integrity isn't enough of a motivator for you to do the right thing, then do it for your own health. At the end of the day, you will be able to look in the mirror and you'll be able to sleep soundly at night.

Blame yourself if you have no branches or leaves;
don't accuse the sun of partiality.

CHINESE PROVERB

24
Be Honest

I HAVE several friends who are younger than me, and I try to counsel them in their relationships, hoping to help them avoid some of the disastrous mistakes I made. One piece of advice: Do not marry until you are thirty. I believe most of us don't have an inkling of who we *really* are until we're about thirty years old. Until then, we usually aren't being honest with others or ourselves. We spend a lot of energy trying to please our parents or attempting to become the perfect employee. I have countless human behavior reports that reflect the stress people endure when they try to be someone they aren't. Are you being honest with yourself?

I went on a self-discovery tour right after my mother's death, and I discovered all sorts of things about myself. I realized that I was hiding God-given qualities simply because I felt using them wasn't what people in my life wanted. No wonder I had a stress-related illness at the time! God made each of us special and unique. Do not be afraid to be true to yourself.

The less we hide our authentic self, the more honest we will be with others, which will build stronger relationships. In the end, we feel happier, more content, and at peace. Isn't that worth a little effort?

No matter what your age, take the time to get to know yourself. Start honoring areas of yourself that perhaps you have locked away in fear. Maybe you will try something new. Surprises may await you! Enjoy the process and the new you!

*No man can produce great things
who is not thoroughly sincere in
dealing with himself.*

JAMES RUSSELL LOWELL

25
Be Assertive. . . Yet Kind

SOMEWHERE in our history, the word "assertive" has gotten a bad rap. When we hear the word, we immediately envision someone steamrolling over others to get his or her way. That isn't being assertive—it's being a jerk. Any behavior taken to an extreme becomes a negative. I believe too many people have gone too far on the "meekness" scale and are, therefore, stuffing resentment and bitterness. Again, taken to an extreme, not standing up for one's self becomes a negative issue.

Emotions are amazing. They are ever changing. If we do not spend time understanding them, they can control us. They can also get us in a heap of trouble. Those who push aside their feelings to the point of being completely submissive to the world are the people who end up shooting their coworkers and killing themselves. Our emotions will affect our spirit positively or negatively. I suggest we become more assertive.

I once told a friend that some people's answering machines *should* say, "Hi, this is Fred. I'm not answering my phone because I don't want to. Don't expect me to call back because I really don't want to talk to you. Have a nice day."

That's a little extreme, but I would much rather know the truth than leave a message and never get a returned call. How are you behaving? Are you going through motions, or are you being true?

Being assertive simply means being open, direct, and honest. I call it "managing expectations" when I work with clients. Do not say you will have something completed by the end of the day when you will probably get it to them tomorrow afternoon. Shoot straight. Assertiveness also works with what we need emotionally. We are responsible to express our needs, but for some reason, we expect people to read our minds and perform. If you are married, you know what I am talking about. Our spouses cannot do something for us if they don't know we want or need it. Be assertive. Tell them!

Because I come from a background of conditional love, I need to hear that my husband plans to be with me forever. I have communicated this need to him, and he is sensitive to my feelings. He makes sure he not only tells me that he loves me, but that he emphasizes that our love will last forever. Just a few extra words have made a world of difference for me. But, I wouldn't get these words if I hadn't assertively expressed myself.

Don't let your emotions build up. Don't stuff feelings inside because you think being quiet is more mature. In many cases, speaking up is the

healthier course to take. Know what you want and
need, then communicate those needs with love.

Be like a postage stamp.
Stick to something until you get there!

JOSH BILLINGS

26
Dare to Be Different

I THANK God that we are all uniquely created. What a boring place it would be if we were all the same. In studying human behavior, I have come to appreciate the different temperaments. We are a blend of all aspects, but we tend to operate primarily in one. God knew what He was doing when He split us up and provided variety. I mean, can you see the world with everyone being like Robin Williams or Jim Carrey? Whoa! That scares me! Or, what about a world full of analytical accountants? Spontaneity may go out the window! Even though we know it "takes all kinds to make the world go around," many people spend their entire lives trying to be someone else. In many cases, past emotional hurts push us to fit in rather than to be set apart. Oh, the stress we put upon ourselves!

The highest courage is to dare to appear to be what one is.

JOHN LANCASTER SPALDING

Be true to yourself! Do not conform simply to fit in, especially when we "are not of this world." We live in this world, but we should be living by a higher standard. Have the courage to stand up for what you know is right. Be yourself. God made you special. Your life is a gift from God. Your gift back to Him is living as the person He intended you to be, not what Hollywood, work, or the world says you should be. Dare to be different!

*Courage comes from acting courageously
on a day-by-day basis.*

BRIAN TRACY

27
Express Yourself

AS TECHNOLOGY increases, our interaction with others decreases. We spend more and more time with inanimate objects and less time connecting with each other. We were not designed for isolation; yet we are creating a world in which we do not feel, and we certainly do not express our emotions. No wonder we are stressed, tired, and sick.

It may be uncomfortable at first, but I encourage you to start talking more and letting yourself be heard. When we show our "human" side, people respond differently to us. Too many folks walk around so "plugged in" to technology that they look and act like robots.

You can begin by expressing your opinions. Think of your thoughts and feelings as an onion: Remove one layer and another is there. Keep peeling! The more you peel away, the more approachable you become. That is when you can connect with people.

Creativity is especially expressed in the ability to make connections, to make associations, to turn things around and express them in a new way.

TIM HANSEN

28
Get in Touch with Yourself

WE ARE SUCH complicated beings. Part of the complication stems from our emotions. They are instrumental in making us whole. They are what make us so different from any other creature. Yet, we tend to discard our feelings, writing them off as a nuisance. On the contrary, they are vital, my friend, and we must understand ourselves—including emotions—if we want to be healthy and strong.

Have you realized yet that living a healthy, balanced, and spiritual life isn't easy? Don't get discouraged because all of your efforts *will* pay off. The reward for living a mediocre life is sickness and stress. But we were designed for greatness!

Dr. Phil says it so well: "Do *whatever* it takes to live a better life." A great place to start is getting to know ourselves.

Ninety percent of the world's woe
comes from people not knowing themselves,
their abilities, their frailties,
and even their real virtues.
Most of us go almost all the way through life
as complete strangers to ourselves.

SYDNEY J. HARRIS

Spend time in quiet and get in touch with your deeper side. Go beyond the façade that you display for the world. Push past the ego and other mechanisms designed to protect you from pain. Look yourself in the eye. You may not like what you see, but it is a place to start. You cannot begin to address a problem if you won't admit you have one. You may have just let the world beat you down. Rise up and claim your life! It was given to you, and you have so much potential. When you start to realize that and step toward living *your* life, you will feel the peace and serenity.

When a man begins to understand himself,
he begins to live.

NORVIN G. McGRANAHAN

SECTION II

REGROUPING OUR MINDS

29
Take a Nap

THE HUSTLE and bustle of the world won't slow down for you. We kid ourselves when we say, "I'll rest just as soon as I finish this project" or "As soon as things calm down, I'll take a break." We will never find a good time to take a break. Life presses on. We must, therefore, take charge!

When we physically exert ourselves, our bodies can quickly recover simply by stopping whatever we're doing. Our mind, on the other hand, requires rest. The mind is constantly gathering information, sorting it, processing it, organizing it, and structuring it. So it's important to rest our minds through sleep. It is very important to get the proper amount of sleep our bodies require. Unfortunately, life doesn't always let us get what we need, so we take what we can get. The beauty of a nap is that a short one can do a world of wonders for us!

I have a friend who has an extended lunch period of an hour and a half. He naps for forty-five minutes and still has time to eat and get back to work. He finds that this reduces his level of stress, gives him a positive outlook on the afternoon, and he has more energy for his evening.

Take twenty minutes to snooze midday if you need. Personally, I love a Sunday afternoon nap for a couple of hours. I am recharging the batteries and preparing for the week ahead. Don't think about it—just do it.

Some people are so nervous that
they keep the coffee awake at night.

ANONYMOUS

30
Learn to Say No and
Give Yourself Permission to Say Yes

FAR TOO often, we create our own stress by saying a simple three-letter word: "Yes." Our heart may be in the right place when we say, "Sure, I'd be happy to make 300 dozen cookies for the school bazaar." Our motives may be pure when we agree to lead an eight-week small group study at the church on our only free night of the week, but saying "yes" to everything and everyone causes additional stress. . . stress that is unnecessary!

Women are especially trained from a very early age to please everyone. We are the ones to comfort and nurture, which requires thinking of others before ourselves. What a wonderful God-given trait! However, do you remember the story of Mary and Martha in Luke Chapter 10? Martha was trying to please everyone and failed to slow down to realize she was in the presence of God's only Son. Mary sat at His feet, and it was enough.

"Martha, Martha," the Lord answered,
"you are worried and upset about many things,
but only one thing is needed.

*Mary has chosen what is better,
and it will not be taken away from her."*

LUKE 10:41–42

Life presents too many circumstances we really don't have any control over, so when we can control the circumstances, we must be strong. We must be honest with ourselves and say "no" when we mean it, not "yes." Protect the areas of your life that are important to you, and don't fall into the trap of overcommitting. If you are in the habit of saying "yes" all the time, I encourage you to practice saying "no" without being rude and without feeling guilty. Say, "No." Try it again one more time: "No." How did that feel?

Now, back to the story about poor Martha. Besides failing to say "no" to things that didn't matter. . .unimportant tasks that could wait. . .she didn't give herself permission to say "yes."

For some of us, saying "yes" to the *right* things can be even more difficult than saying "no." Prioritize your life and honor those things first. The more you speak the truth to yourself and others, the less stress you will impose upon yourself and the healthier your life will become.

Say what you mean, and mean what you say!

ANONYMOUS

31
Write Out Your Goals

WE HAVE all heard the saying "running around like a chicken with its head cut off"—and we've probably illustrated that concept at some time. In other words, we are running around in circles, completely confused. Your life might resemble that more than you care to admit, and it is stressing you out. Fear not, we're about to change that.

I have always been a goal-minded individual, and I consider it a gift. Give me anything in the future, and I can organize the necessary steps to get there and outline the possible obstacles along the way. I have found that many people have not inherited this gift, but they *can* learn it.

I'm coaching a woman right now who is great at making goals and even writing them down, but she doesn't break them into manageable pieces. She, therefore, gets overwhelmed by the goal and doesn't have a high rate of success in achieving it. Then she faces frustration, disappointment, and stress. Can you relate?

> *You'll never hit the target*
> *if you don't have a goal.*
>
> STEVEN R. SMITH

Make an effort to look at your goals and put some legs to them. If they are important enough to you, then you must write them down. Once you have them on paper, then "chunk them down" into smaller goals. Again, you have heard the old saying, "How do you eat an elephant? One bite at a time!" It works. As you conquer one small piece at a time, you will gain momentum as you move closer to achieving your goal. Before you know it, you will get to your destination without much stress at all.

"If I'm not here, I'm lost.
I've gone to look for myself.
If I should return before I get back,
please have me wait."

ANONYMOUS

32
Write Your Personal Mission Statement

WE HAVE probably all asked the soul-searching question: Why am I here? I wonder how many of us have actually done the homework to find the answer? I don't know about you, but I lack peace when I am without purpose. I am restless, uneasy, and tense. So, several years ago, I decided to write a personal mission statement—one I could live by each and every day.

A personal mission statement includes your values, but it goes beyond that to describe your gifts, talents, contributions, and calling. Why are you here? Find out, write it down, and passionately live it. You will feel better.

You don't get to choose how you're going to die. Or when. You can only decide how you're going to live.

JOAN BAEZ

33
Manage the Mundane Tasks of Life Well

SOMEONE once asked me why I am a time management nut, and I quickly responded that it's because I want to have fun and enjoy life!

Life is full of mundane tasks and things that must be done. Period. No matter what is going on in our lives, we still must wash, dry, and fold the clothes. No matter how high we climb the corporate ladder of success, most of us will still shop for groceries and pick up the dry cleaning. Whether you are a clean freak or a slob, you still spend time maintaining your home and caring for your yard.

The list goes on, doesn't it? And all of these items can, and often do, cause us stress. My philosophy, therefore, has been to get these chores done as quickly and efficiently as possible and then move on to the "finer things in life" like having fun. Why be disorganized at the grocery store and take twice as long finding everything when you can create a list and have a plan that will leave more time for you to do something you *enjoy.* Maybe you get excited about cleaning the house, but most of us would rather have a fairy pop in and do it for us. Since a fairy isn't an option, schedule time to dust one day and tackle the floors on another.

Don't delay the inevitable chores. Procrastination only leads to more stress. Instead, stay focused on the task at hand, and you'll finish more quickly than if you take on too many different projects at one time. Managing life's chores more effectively will reduce your stress and create extra time for *you!*

*Great things are not done by impulse
but by a series of small things brought together.*

Vincent van Gogh

34
Create "Buffers" in Your Schedule

Has your schedule ever been so full that you don't have time to hit the bathroom? When we fill up our calendars to the point of boiling over, it is stressful. What a horrible feeling to rush from one appointment to another—especially when you didn't schedule enough time in between and are constantly late and feeling harried. And once you are late, you never seem to catch up. It can be exhausting! Can you relate?

I have a better way called "buffers." A buffer is a little break or cushion between things. In your day, a buffer would be time blocked out to allow "room for error" such as running late from a previous meeting. Instead of backing everything up tight, try the buffer zone. If you need it, you will have that extra fifteen or twenty minutes to get where you need to go without being late. If you don't need it, then consider the extra fifteen or twenty minutes a blessing! You can get something done ahead of schedule or simply relax. Try it; you'll like it.

Simplicity, simplicity, simplicity!
I say, let your affairs be as two or three,
and not a hundred or a thousand. . .
Simplify, simplify.

HENRY DAVID THOREAU

35
Plan Your Work and Work Your Plan

YOU HAVE heard the old saying, "If you fail to plan, plan to fail." Going through life without a plan not only reduces our chances of success, but it causes stress for those around us.

Whether at work or on your day off, having some plan of attack will help you get where you want to go. You may not like planning or may consider yourself more spontaneous than that, but planning does have its place. If we are always spontaneous, we may never really do anything. It is great to say, "Let's do lunch," but if you and your friend never actually book it, you may never hook up. But if we plan some things, then we have the time to be flexible and do whatever we like more freely, without anything hanging over our head.

Making plans is just step one, though. You must then follow through with those plans. If you plan to visit Grandma and Grandpa's on Saturday morning, then determine when you will arrive and stick to those plans. Have an idea of approximately how long you will stay and then plan to leave about that time in order to protect some "flexibility" for later in the day. Planning isn't a bad word. It is actually your friend if you let it be.

Time is neither our friend or our enemy;
it is something that gets measured out to us
to see what we will make of it.

RICHARD GAYLORD BRILEY

36
Relax

THOSE WHO knew me a long time ago would be amused to see me writing about relaxation. However, I am a new creation, and you can be, too. . . with some relaxing.

The problem I had with relaxing is that once I actually stopped, I had time to think. When I had to think for awhile, then I would begin to "feel," and with feeling came pain. Keeping busy was my way of avoiding pain. I couldn't even sit still long enough to watch a two-hour movie. Relaxing is a beautiful, soothing thing, and we need it to be healthy. Can you really relax?

Take time to just "be." Don't feel like you have to book every moment of the day with something productive. Don't feel like you have to "be on" all the time, either. Let your hair down, and let it all out in private. The great thing about relaxing is that you don't have to do or be a single thing if you don't want to! So close your eyes and relax.

A heart at peace gives life to the body.

PROVERBS 14:30

37
Make a Candlelight Dinner. . .for Yourself

NO, THIS isn't a romance book, so don't pass this tip! Candles should not be reserved only for creating a romantic atmosphere, but they should also be used to soothe our minds. Look into a warm flame, and you seem to feel better almost instantly. You can feel your stress begin to melt away.

Break out some candles and your fine china and linen, and make yourself a heartwarming, soul-soothing meal. Play your favorite uplifting tunes and toast to all the things you are grateful for in your life. Savor every bite and absorb the richness of the moment. You are in the presence of a special person. . .you!

Happiness is a conscious choice,
not an automatic response.
MILDRED BARTHEL

38
Listen to Soothing Music

DO YOU know how powerful your mind is? You can literally become whatever you spend time thinking about. If you are worrying about overdue projects, car pools, and an impossible calendar, you feed your mind negative thoughts. These thoughts, in turn, create your behavior. The more stress we take into our minds, the more stressed out we act.

We cannot tune out all stress, but we can control what we allow in. Take music, for example. We are blessed with a variety of styles and talented artists, but all music is not created equal. Some types preach a negative, destructive message while others are filled with hope, peace, and love. What are you listening to?

Tune into music that reaches your heart.

I don't know about you, but I'd rather fill myself with positive, soothing tunes that will create balance in my mind and result in more pleasant actions. Remember, your actions *do* speak louder than words, so tune into music that reaches your heart.

Sing and make music

in your heart to the Lord.

EPHESIANS 5:19

39
Read a Fun Book

I WAS NOT an avid reader as a young person. My mother tried to get me to read, but to no avail. Through time, I did learn to love self-improvement and business books. My bookshelves are full of secrets to success, tips for time management, and advice from all walks of life. More recently, however, I have come to truly appreciate reading just for relaxation.

Feeling a bit frustrated and stressed? Pick up a fun, easy-to-read, brainless book with a good story and read it. Try different styles of books to see which ones entertain you the most.

Want to take it up another notch? Sit outside or lie in the sun while you read. Turn off the world and its worries and dive into the plot—get carried away for moments in time. The world will still be there when you return—but you'll feel much better!

Of all the things I have lost,
I miss my mind the most.

ANONYMOUS

40
Read a Nourishing Book

WHEN I was young, my mother loved romance novels. Nothing turns my stomach quicker than a gushy, sappy tale. But when I discovered practical, life-changing books, I began to read. I discovered that I didn't despise all books; I just disliked certain genres. Reading is good for our minds, and it keeps us sharp.

Talk with someone who is retired and that person will tell you the importance of keeping his or her mind active. The old philosophy "Use it or lose it" applies to our brain cells at any age. The more alert our minds, the better equipped they will be to handle the pressures of life.

Read often. Challenge yourself with books that explore different cultures or ones that present historical events. Engulf yourself in books that uncover new theories, philosophies, or medical breakthroughs. Whatever your taste, interest, or flavor, read.

The more you read, the more you know. The more you know, the more aware you will become of the world around you, and that prepares you to handle more situations. The more prepared you are for life, the less stress you will experience. And you know what? By reading this book, you are making the first steps. Bravo!

The mind is a terrible thing to waste.

ANONYMOUS

41
Look Through Old Scrapbooks or Photo Albums

I HAVE fond memories of being a child on New Year's Eve with my parents. Our tradition was to look at old photo albums until midnight. We would usually start with baby pictures and work up to the present day. We would laugh and reminisce about "the good old days," which seemed so pleasant and carefree. Now and then, it is good to go back.

We can all get caught up in the "here and now" and the stress that accompanies each day. I believe a good stroll down memory lane is healthy once in awhile. I am constantly amazed at how fond most of our memories are of the past. My mom was right; memories do become richer with time. And, they usually have wisdom and lessons to teach us.

Do not fear death but
be afraid of the unlived life.

TUCK EVERLASTING
Disney Movie

When was the last time you picked up a photo

album or scrap album? Why do we save all of that stuff if we don't peruse it now and then? Get a nice cup of tea or hot cocoa, sit on a comfy couch, and "stroll." You may find yourself smiling and laughing out loud. . . . I hope you do.

❧

*Memories become fonder
the more time that passes.*

MILDRED S. BOSSÉ

42
Hang Out in a Hammock

I THOUGHT about including a "release of liability" for this suggestion. Hammocks are tricky! To sit in a hammock often requires a skill that I lack. I have difficulty "gracefully" climbing in and settling down. But sitting in it is worth the struggle. The cradle of a hammock provides true rest.

If you have already begun to apply some of the tips in this book, this one is great to combine with others like reading or taking a nap. It lends itself well to many more creative ways to de-stress. Use your imagination. Just be careful climbing out!

Find rest, O my soul, in God alone;
my hope comes from him.

PSALM 62:5

43
Take a Sunday Afternoon Drive in the Country

I AM BLESSED to live in beautiful, sunny, southern California. So many of the car commercials on TV are filmed on the California coast or in the rolling hills and vineyards. I love driving. Many times, my most creative thoughts come from time on the open road.

Let me say that I hate traffic; I think we all do. It is frustrating to say the least. I certainly don't recommend for anyone to deliberately pull onto a congested freeway. Do your best to try and find a road that will offer some tranquility and scenery. Although I love cranking my tunes up while driving, when I have complete silence in the car, God speaks to me in the most profound ways. Out on the open road, the farther from home I get, the farther my troubles seem. Driving gives us time to think, process, and reflect; and it gives us perspective.

Struggling with an issue? Really uptight? Grab a bottle of water, a light jacket, your keys, your sunglasses, and cruise in the country. Turn off that cell phone. Disconnect. Become one with the road for awhile and see where it takes you.

Sunday afternoons were meant for driving!

44
Have a Hobby

HOBBIES provide an outlet for creativity that perhaps we don't get to use in the normal course of the day. Hobbies also keep us from falling into ruts of boredom in front of the television. And hobbies can get us in touch with ourselves and reduce stress.

You may already have a hobby and know exactly what you love to do in your spare time. I wasn't sure I had a hobby. I don't like knitting or crocheting. I am not much of an artist, so painting, sculpting, and pottery didn't appeal to me. I began to feel "hobby-challenged" until I dug deeper. What did I truly love? People.

I love doing things for people. Whether it is making cards or baking a special dessert, I love creating gifts to express my feelings for those I care about. I also enjoy living an active lifestyle. I realized that these pastimes are hobbies for me. The more time I spend making a gift for someone or the more time I share about wellness with others, the more energized I become. It is a creative outlet for me, and it certainly is a stress buster!

What do you like to do? Don't be afraid to try something new. You might actually discover a hidden talent! Remember, all work and no play can make us grumpy!

Learn the craft of knowing how
to open your heart
and to turn on your creativity.
There's a light inside of you.

JUDITH JAMISON

45
Get Organized!

WE HAVE chuckled at the ironic saying "An organized desk is the sign of a sick mind." But, unfortunately, the opposite is usually true. Our emotions and thoughts tend to reflect our surroundings. The more disorganized our home or office, the more fragmented our mind. Peace comes from some type of order.

God made each of us uniquely, and we all have different styles. How wonderful! The world would be a boring place if we were all identical. But get rid of the clutter and clear your mind! If you don't need it and haven't used it for more than six months, give it away. Bless someone else. "One man's trash is another man's treasure" (anonymous).

*A clutter-free counter is the sign
of a clear mind.*

Organize at least those things you use often: spices, tools, address book, clothes, CDs. I don't care what system you use, just pick something that works for you. The more "in place" things are, the clearer your mind will be. Remember, you don't have to be a clean freak—just clutter free!

Have nothing in your homes that
you don't know to be useful
and believe to be beautiful.

WILLIAM MORRIS

46
Watch What You Watch

NOW THAT I have learned the art of slowing down and relaxing, I love a good flick! My husband and I often catch a movie on our date day. We like seeing comedies, dramas, and romances.

I'm not suggesting we watch everything that comes out without any discernment. I advocate screening what we watch based upon the lifestyle we want to live. Being conservative is a far cry from being legalistic. Don't be so narrow that you miss out on some great movies that may lift your spirits or simply make you smile. Be careful, though, to limit the amount of negative images, violence, rage, and other traits that contradict the lifestyle you choose. Remember, "Garbage in, garbage out!" See you at the movies!

Whatever is true, whatever is noble,
whatever is right,
whatever is pure, whatever is lovely,
whatever is admirable—
if anything is excellent or praiseworthy—
think about such things.

PHILIPPIANS 4:8

47
Know Your Limits

MY HUSBAND often teases that the world could come to an end and I wouldn't know it. I don't read the paper, and I don't watch the news. Why? I feel too often the newspaper is filled with negative, depressing stories and the news is a bunch of hype. As the media says, "Tragedies sell and heartwarming stories smell." Accordingly, I can do without being completely in the "know" and really don't need the extra stress.

The ironic thing is that when terrorists attacked our beloved country on September 11, 2001, I knew before my husband. See, if it is truly newsworthy, I *will* find out. Otherwise, I monitor what I will allow to bombard my life and inject stress.

My mother would watch the news for hours on end. She would be concerned about people in the path of a major storm system somewhere in Russia and then not sleep all night because she was worrying about a possible situation arising in Haiti. Did her fret change anything? No. It only reduced the quality of her short life.

The world is large. We can certainly be concerned about what is happening in different counties, regions, states, and countries. But we must discern our level of involvement to manage our stress in a healthy manner. Within the great, wide world, we have our circle of influence.

In the smaller realm, we can truly make a difference, so that's where we should invest our emotions and energies. Certainly, I am not discounting the power of prayer for the larger world! God uses His people to accomplish some mighty things. However, know your limits. Some of us get more stressed than others. If you tend to get stressed more, make deliberate efforts to screen the media's messages of despair. Use good judgment and minimize your stress.

If you worry about what might be,
and wonder what might have been,
you will ignore what is.

ANONYMOUS

48
Celebrate Your Victories and Learn from Your Mistakes

I DON'T know about you, but I don't need help in acknowledging my mistakes and failures. I'm my own worst enemy. I did, however, gain an entirely new outlook on mistakes when I read *The Inner Game of Tennis* by W. Timothy Gallwey. In a nutshell, he tells us to look at mistakes for what they are and to not attach negative associations to ourselves. For instance, if I hit the ball into the net, I just didn't follow through on my stroke. It doesn't mean I'm stupid or that I'm a horrible player; it simply means I didn't follow through on my stroke and made an error. Period. Try to look at your mistakes in a different light. Accept them, take responsibility for them, and then move on!

And don't forget to pause long enough to pat yourself on the back and say, "Good job!" when you have met a goal, confronted a tough issue, or have done something different as a result of a previous mistake. It's okay to say, "I did it!" or "Way to go!" In fact, cheering for yourself is a great stress reducer. We can be in such a hurry to reach the next goal or accomplish the next task that we forget to pause, reflect, and enjoy. Go ahead, jump over the net. . . you know you want to!

Only he who does nothing makes no mistakes.

FRENCH PROVERB

49
Discover the Champion in You!

Man is what he believes.

ANTON CHEKHOV

"GOD DOESN'T make garbage," someone once said, and I agree. I don't know you, but I can tell you that you are special! In fact, you are a champion! Do you believe that?

You have been given so many talents; do not waste them. You have been given life; do not forsake it. You have been given a heart and soul; listen to them. Discover the champion in you! Trust and believe.

*Your success depends mainly upon
what you think of yourself
and whether you believe in yourself.*

WILLIAM J. H. BOETCKER

50
Don't Hold Back

Be all that you can be.

U. S. Army

CHILDREN are free to express every range of emotion. If they are excited, they shriek! If they are happy, they giggle. If they are sad, they cry. If they are mad, they stomp their feet.

Along life's journey, though, we begin to believe that part of the "maturing" process is suppressing emotions. Before you know it, our spirit is dead before our hair even grays! Keeping things inside causes stress. We've got to let it out and live!

Please don't think I'm supporting inappropriate outbursts of anger. You should know better anyway. But I am encouraging you to not hold back when you need to express yourself. I have given up trying to be strong during sentimental commercials. I certainly do not bawl and fall to pieces, but I get teary-eyed. It is a good thing. Holding emotions inside creates destructive barriers. It builds walls between us and God or those we love. Life is too short to live in disharmony.

Make sure you show some enthusiasm in this thing called life. When was the last time you jumped for joy? Free your emotions and rid yourself of negative stress. Give life what you've got!

❧

*What counts is not necessarily
the size of the dog in the fight,
but the size of the fight in the dog.*

DWIGHT D. EISENHOWER

51
Choose Wisely

LIFE IS full of choices and opportunities. Sometimes, too many choices can overwhelm us, but we usually appreciate the options. When we do finally select something, we have decided against everything else—we call this "opportunity cost." For example, if you attend your son's baseball game after work, you have chosen *not* to spend that hour cleaning house, cooking dinner, reading, or anything else. You made him your priority. And that is a wise choice. You probably would not feel stress from this decision; rather, you would feel connected by supporting your son.

Choose wisely.

Some choices, though, are not as positive and can cause stress. Take, for instance, a report that is due at work tomorrow, and you haven't finished it yet. It is 5:00 P.M., and you have plans to catch a movie with a friend. What do you decide? Do you stay late to finish the report or keep your plans? By staying late to get your job done, you will eliminate stress—but you let a friend down. Each decision has a cost.

Life is fleeting and is all about choice. Choose wisely.

Decide on what is right,
and stick to it.

GEORGE ELIOT

52
Control Technology

OKAY, I AM going to date myself here. I remember the days when computers were going to run the world and we would live in a paperless society. Technology was supposed to "save" us and make life easier, less complicated, and certainly less stressful. *Ha!* I'd laugh more, but it really isn't funny. Technology, instead, has isolated us, stressed us out, and is controlling our lives—not to mention generating enormous amounts of paper.

Technology is a wonderful invention. But, we must put it in its place. Cell phones are great for emergencies, but they shouldn't be permanently glued to our ears! Turn your phones off, especially when you are with someone at a restaurant, a movie, or doing anything. Forgo the pagers and the compulsive need to answer every single phone call—that is why we have voice mail. Don't stop what you're doing and check your E-mail just because you heard those infamous words, "You've got mail!" Block out certain times of the day to respond to E-mail so you don't become an E-mail addict.

Tame the E-mail monster!

As you turn some technology off, tune into life. Look around you. Take deep breaths. Listen. . .ah, the sound of nature, and I don't mean the Discovery Channel.

❧

Find what things you can
have some control over,
and come up with
creative ways to take control.

DR. PAUL ROSCH

53
Think Positively

THE MIND is an incredible tool. It has the power to take us to great heights we never imagined or to unbearably low pits of despair. What you think, you will become. What I call "tapes" are constantly playing in our heads. Depending upon what your tapes say, you may be at peace or extremely unhappy.

If you're thinking negatively about yourself ("I'm too fat; I'm ugly; I'm stupid."), try replacing those messages with something positive ("I'm a good person; I'm loved by God; I'm smart."). Also watch your word choices. Rather than saying you have a huge problem, state that you have a challenge to overcome. With the latter phrasing, your mind will assume more of a positive outcome. Do not use the word "hate"; instead say you have difficulty with something. And never say you "can't" because we all know that with God, all things are possible! Think about that!

Think you can, think you can't;
either way, you'll be right.

HENRY FORD

54
Live in the Moment

WE LIVE in a fast-paced society in which everything is on the go, and multitasking has been taken to new levels. But by doing so much, do we really do anything well? I only know that the faster the treadmill speed of your life, the more you will deal with high levels of stress.

I actually enjoy the treadmill. The predetermined speed challenges me to go a little farther and faster than I might on my own. However, we must turn it off and "live in the moments" of life when they come.

Slow the hectic treadmill of survival or turn it off so you won't miss the precious moments of life that come your way. When you are with your friend, be with him. When you are having dinner with your spouse, enjoy the meal and conversation. When you are on vacation, don't take work with you. Don't fall into the trap of multitasking yourself right out of important moments. Be there: body, mind, heart, and soul.

*A happy person is not a person
in a certain set of circumstances,
but rather a person with
a set of attitudes.*

HUGH DOWNS

55
Read the Comics

ALTHOUGH I'm not a big fan of reading the newspaper, the comic pages are an entirely different story! Talk about a stress buster!

Dig them out and read them. Laugh out loud! Cut out the ones that are "keepers" and file them in your desk drawer for those days when you need a pick-me-up. Okay, did you read the one where. . . ?

Don't worry, be happy.

ANONYMOUS

56
Live with Purpose

IT IS NOT enough to just find out "why you are here," but you must decide to live out your purpose. If you are not aligned with where you should be and where God wants you to be, you feel stress.

We can all think of times in life when we were at peace. At the time, we were probably living our purpose. Have you ever had a job that didn't match your talents or personality? Talk about being *out* of alignment and tense! I believe God truly wants us to be happy and feel fulfilled.

If you can't find your purpose, look at your passions and hobbies. These are usually good indicators of what we enjoy, are good at, and are happy doing. Dig deeper, though. Pray and reflect. Ask God, "What would *You* have me do?" and then wait for the answer. Alas, you will discover your true self and live with purpose and passion. Peace be with you.

Where there is no vision, the people perish.

PROVERBS 29:18 KJV

SECTION III

REENERGIZING OUR BODIES

57
Take a Hot Bubble Bath

STRESS is the body's physical and chemical reaction to life's events. A huge percentage of all doctor visits are a result of stress. Our bodies can only take so much, so we must pamper them occasionally. Soothing the body will reduce the results of stress and help you manage challenges better.

Work your fingers to the bones
and all you will get is bony fingers.

ANONYMOUS

Last year, my husband and I built a deck off of our master bedroom and installed a glorious hot tub on it. I thought I would never take another hot bath again, but I was wrong. Although I love hitting the spa (another tension tamer), taking a hot bubble bath still relaxes me in a different way. I think I like the ambiance I can create for my bath.

First, I block out time when I know my day will be quiet—free of interruptions and phone calls. I then light a bunch of candles around the tub. Depending on my mood, I will play soothing instrumental music or just enjoy the silence. I make sure the temperature is "comfortably uncomfortable." I then sink in and let the bubbles do their magic.

Okay, so the bubbles aren't magic, but they provide a great environment for my body to heal. A hot soak helps the body heal itself while relaxing the mind and spirit. Use bath time as a time to reflect, pray, meditate, or doze off. Sometimes I'll even read.

Experiment with scented and herbal bubble baths. Lavender is known for relaxing and chamomile is very soothing. Look for something that treats your skin with conditioner, too. You may also want to try a variety of candle fragrances. I personally like lavender bubble bath with vanilla candles.

Remember, hot baths aren't just for kids or women. Everybody can benefit from a hot soak and detoxification. Take the plunge! If you aren't used to staying still for long, you will probably get out of the tub while the water is still warm. If, however, you are a hot bubble bath professional, you may have to add more hot water to keep it comfortable. Now that is my kind of stress!

Any time I am stressed, I take a long, hot bath.
I've been in the tub since last Tuesday.

ANONYMOUS

58
Care for Your Skin

I AM FAIRLY new to the spa scene. In fact, last summer, my husband treated me to a couple of visits to the local spa, and that was my first experience. The esthetician carefully cleansed my face, removing all dirt and residue. She then examined my skin with a magnifying glass, looking for trouble areas to work on. I was pleasantly surprised when she said, "There is nothing for me to do!" I had very healthy skin. I guess the years of living in a dry climate paid off. Research shows that people in dryer climates have less skin damage and wrinkles than those in humid climates. Why? Because those of us in dry climates have to put moisturizer on our skin. People in humid climates either forget or don't think it is important to add moisturizers to their skin since it is damp. Our skin, no matter where we live, needs to be cared for regularly. If we don't, it will show. If we are stressed, it will definitely show.

Zits, bumps, and cold sores are all, to some degree, reactions to stress (and our eating habits and genes). If you suffer from any of these, it may be your body's way of warning: "I'm overloaded! Something must change." If you don't listen, things will only get worse. So care for your face and help it remove the toxins.

You don't have to pay a fortune for a facial. Many people who work at hair salons charge reasonable prices. At a spa resort, you will pay for the name and atmosphere. You should also be taking care of your skin every day, whether you're a man or woman. Remember if you have skin, you need to care for it! Cleanse your face every morning and night. People with oily skin may need to freshen up midday. Use a toner that helps your skin balance back out. And then moisturize, moisturize, moisturize! The healthier your skin, the better it can process toxins. The more you care for your skin, the better it will look. And, it is the only skin we are given, so we need to make it last.

Use sunscreen! We all need to remember this. The older I get, the more sensitive to the sun my skin becomes. And our world is more polluted than it used to be. Our skin needs protection from the harmful ultraviolet rays. I use foundation base makeup and facial lotion with SPF in it so that I don't have to remember—it's taken care of first thing in the morning. Your skin is already processing your worry and anxieties. Give it a break! Cover it up with SPF 15 or higher.

When things get tough,

the tough get a facial!

59
Breathe

WHEN I was young, my mother, like yours, always harped on me to stand up straight. She insisted that I have good posture, but never told me why. Not until I got extensively involved in the health and fitness industry did I learn the importance of good posture: healthy breathing. When we are hunched over, we restrict our lungs and force them to operate at only half capacity. When our bodies do not get enough oxygen, they don't run at full speed. Therefore, we are setting ourselves up for stress and sickness.

Our breathing is paramount to our state of being. When we feel stressed, we tend to take shorter, faster breaths from the chest instead of the abdomen. The more we breathe like this, the tenser we become. The more uptight we are, the more hyper and shallow our breathing becomes. However, you can manage your stress by concentrating on good breathing techniques.

Breathe deep from your abdomen,
not your chest.

Before every fitness class I instruct, I remind participants to breathe deeply from their abdomen, not their chest. One way to ensure this is to lower the shoulders and, you guessed it, stand or sit up nice and tall. Relaxing our upper body provides the environment our lungs and heart need to breathe easily. The more oxygen we have in our system, the better our bodies will perform.

Here's a great exercise you can do anywhere to immediately reduce your anxiety:

- Take in a deep breath for a count of 15.
- Hold that breath for a count of 20.
- Release the breath over the count of 10, pursing your lips and pushing the air out.
- Take a regular breath in for the count of 5.
- Repeat one to four times.

WARNING:

You may relax to the point of wanting to sleep! If I have trouble sleeping at night, I will repeat this exercise about ten times and by then I'm asleep. Doing this two to four times should fix you right up and enable you to manage whatever you are facing

with confidence and strength. Breathing. . .
it gives quality of life!

*The answer to stress management is to realize that
stress is an unavoidable consequence of life.*

DR. PAUL ROSCH

60
Smile

DID YOU know that your body uses fewer muscles to smile than it does to frown? Yet, we tend to be down in the mouth far too often. I've often wondered what visitors think when they walk into a church. The message tells them how loving God is, but all the congregants have pained looks on their faces. What happened to showing God's love with a smile? I think God would like us to smile more, don't you agree? We really are blessed. We should show it!

Facial expressions are no different than our body posture or our thoughts. If our face is grim, our attitudes and emotions will follow. We will focus on negative aspects of our lives. But if we "put on a happy face," our mood will follow. We will turn our thoughts toward our blessings and be grateful. I know doing this can feel fake at times, but staying in a negative state only hurts your health. Besides, smiling reflects love.

Try to smile more at life's little quirks. Instead of blowing up, try turning up the corners of your mouth. Rather than shooting laser darts from your eyes at a coworker who is driving you nuts, send him or her a smile. Take the time to smile when you are happy. Too often, we hurry the content moments of life along so we can rush on to the next challenge. Wait! Hold on. Pause and smile.

People are drawn to smiles more than they are attracted to intense or serious expressions. Smiling is also like laughter: It is contagious. Be a carrier and a catalyst for change!

May you always have a smile on your face
and laughter in your heart.

ANONYMOUS

61
Walk

FITNESS trends come and go. You might even have a few pieces of cardio equipment collecting dust somewhere in your garage or attic. We continually seem to take a simple principle and make it complicated. Want to simplify your life and still stay healthy? Walk.

Walking is great for our bodies! Unlike jogging or running, it is easy on the joints. It uses our legs, elongating and toning the muscles. It requires our arms to create momentum, and most importantly, it uses our heart. Walking also de-stresses us. Combine it with talking with a close friend or your spouse, and you have a winning combination for improved health.

As a society, we do not get enough cardio exercise to significantly impact our health. And when we do get on the treadmill or hit the streets, we aren't working hard enough. I don't know about you, but if I'm going to dedicate the time to exercise, I want to get the most out of it. So we need to make sure we're working the heart enough to keep it clean and strong.

Here's a chart that indicates the levels of work and gives you an idea of how to know and monitor your level of exertion:

LEVEL OF WORK DESCRIPTION

1.0   Easy–Very light—Breathing through nose.
2.0   Light—Breathing fuller through nose.
3.0   Slightly moderate—Breathing begins to change.
4.0   Moderate—Breathing through mouth.
5.0   Strong—Labored but controlled breathing.
6.0   Hard—Labored but controlled breathing. "Comfortably uncomfortable."
7.0   Very hard—Labored, heavier breathing.
8.0   Very, very hard—Labored, heavier breathing.
9.0   Extremely hard—Begin breathlessness.
10.0 Maximum effort—Complete breathlessness.

When you walk, work minimally at level 5.0. for 20 minutes. Preferably and ideally, you should work at level 6.0, which is "comfortably uncomfortable." In other words, you know you are working hard, but you can sustain it for the 20 minutes. You will be looking at your watch and timing the 20 minutes because it is work! You then want to spend 10 minutes challenging yourself at level 7.0 and 8.0. This is what will eventually improve your cardio capacity or VO2 max (ability for the body to process and use oxygen). For those who are physically ready, visit level 9.0 and 10.0 briefly, maybe right at the very end of your walk.

CAUTION: Make sure you cool down gradually when you're done with your walking workout. You never want to just "stop" from a high level of effort. And, when in doubt, check it out. If you aren't sure you're ready for physical exertion, visit your physician.

Our legs were made to walk. It is a natural movement for us. With all you can gain from a nice walk outside, what are you waiting for?

⁓

Want to reduce your risk of heart attack?
Walk four times a week.

AMERICAN HEART ASSOCIATION

62
Eat Your Fruits and Vegetables

HAVE YOU ever seen the commercial that shows a woman leaving the bakery and her buns are "cinnamon buns"? The slogan is: "You are what you eat." Haven't our mothers told us this our entire lives? I think we conveniently forget that vital piece of information. We put some scary stuff in our bodies; yet we are surprised when our body breaks down on us.

Most people would not put anything but gasoline in their cars because they understand that the motor needs the proper fuel to perform. Our bodies are no different. Without the proper nutrition, they don't function properly. Add stress to that and the body is in trouble. And that's when illness strikes. I know we hate to admit that "Mom knows best," but she is right. Eat your fruits and veggies.

The recommendation for a healthy, well-balanced diet is 70 servings of fruits and vegetables a week. What constitutes a serving? A medium-sized piece of fruit is 1 serving and so is a cup of lettuce. You can eat canned and frozen fruits and vegetables, but they do have less nutritional value, more sugar and chemicals, and your portion size is smaller (½ cup).

I love fruit and vegetables, so I easily eat my daily

quota. I understand, though, that you may not be a veggie fan. If you value your health, I suggest that you find a creative way to start enjoying fruits and vegetables. Your body needs them to survive. Replace nutritionally empty snacks—such as cookies—with fruit, and add a salad to your lunch and dinners. I make a big salad that we then eat from for days. It stays nicely in the refrigerator as long as you drain all the excess water during preparation. My husband slices up fruit that we can dish out at any time. Convenience is always a factor for us, isn't it? Do what it takes. I know someone wants you to be around for a very long time.

You are what you eat.

ANONYMOUS

63
Reduce Sweets

UNTIL NOW, you've been able to appreciate the ideas and stress management tips I have offered. But perhaps to suggest that you eliminate dessert from your diet is going too far! I'm certainly not implying that we need to rid our bodies of all tasty treats (I like certain desserts now and then), but we must watch what we take in. Stress makes it difficult; I'll be honest with you. The more stress you have, the more you will crave things that aren't good for you. The more you eat sweets and fattening foods, the less your body can retard stress. It's a vicious cycle—not to mention that stress can cause serious weight gain in a hurry. To prevent making matters worse, I encourage you to make wise choices.

I remember when one product line came out that advertised that it only offered healthy foods. Suddenly my mom, who didn't like any sweets, was eating their cookies because they were "healthy." "Hey, they said it was good for me, so it must be true," she reasoned. She wasn't the only one to be suckered into a less healthy lifestyle through this innovative marketing tactic.

Unfortunately, many people still believe what they

see on television. The sooner we realize that most ad-
vertisements *are* manipulative, the better off we all will
be. I mean, what is their motive? Your health? Hardly!
They advertise their product to make money. . .and
lots of it! If something claims to be "fat free," it is
probably high in sugar, which you don't need. You
are trading one "evil" for another. Sugar and caffeine
will intensify your stress, not make it better. They are
not soothing agents but stimulating ones. Make better choices!

Limit your sweet intake to five portions a week.
"Oh, I can do that," you say, "that's easy." Not so fast.
Let's look at what constitutes a "sweet." Do you enjoy low-fat yogurt for breakfast? It's a sweet. . . usually very high in sugar. Do you put jam on your
toast? It's a sweet. Breads and pasta have sugar. Then
of course cookies, cake, pies (the list goes on) are
desserts or sweets. It all adds up and can add inches
to your waistline if you are not careful.

Remember, we should eat to live,
not live to eat.

ANONYMOUS

A good approach is to commit to eliminating
one sweet from your diet. Perhaps you have
indulged in a candy bar at work each day. Get rid of
it! You can cut one item out of your diet and see an

improvement. Then when you feel stronger and more confident, knock another one out. Step by step you can adapt your diet to be healthier. Remember, eat to live—don't live to eat.

❧

Self-love is the only weight-loss aid
that really works in the long run.

JENNY CRAIG

64
Watch Your Fat Intake

MORE THAN 60 percent of Americans are overweight compared to only 10 percent of the French. What do we do that is so different? Besides eating high-fat diets, we eat too much. "Super-sized" meal portions were created because our mentality is "more is better." Other countries are simply content with having any food to eat. But, we want more of everything, so why not food? It's the American way, and it's killing us.

Obesity just doesn't affect our physical health, but also lowers our self-esteem. And when we don't feel good about ourselves, we worry over little things that shouldn't matter. Thus, we enter a vicious cycle. Stress can cause overeating, which leads to being overweight, which results in low self-esteem and more worrying and eating. Can you see the pattern? Perhaps you are living the pattern. You can break it by taking one step: Reduce your fat intake.

One great way to make a huge dent in your fat intake is to swear off fried foods. Period! If that seems too difficult, start by eliminating just one fried item like French fries. Replace fries with a side salad, baked potato, or fruit. When this becomes habit, remove another fried item from your diet, like fried chicken.

Keep removing items one by one, and you will make a significant difference in your fat intake.

Fat should be about 25 to 30 percent of our diet, but no more than 10 percent of that should be saturated fat, which is found in fried foods and oils. That number may sound high, but it quickly adds up when you add butter, sour cream, milk, meats, and any sweets—all of which are high in fat. Many products have low-fat options, but increase your sugar intake. You are better off controlling what you eat than simply looking for a quick fix. When it comes to good health, no miracle solution exists.

We must get our protein, as it is high in vitamins—but look for lean cuts of meat. Butter is okay, but use it sparingly. Try to avoid extras like sour cream and cream cheese, which are basically nutritionally empty and contain a lot of fat. The bottom line is that we need to make wise and healthy choices. The better we control our fat intake, the less likely that we will become overweight. The world certainly bombards us with enough pain, hardship, and stress. Let's not inflict pain upon ourselves. Watch your fat intake! Think healthy.

Everything in moderation.

ANONYMOUS

65
Adjust Your Dairy Intake Accordingly

DEPENDING upon who you talk to, you will get different theories about dairy products. One fact is irrefutable: We are the only species that continues to drink milk once we pass infancy. Many people have intolerance for dairy products. Dairy is one of the top three culprits for causing snoring and breathing problems, and dairy is difficult for our bodies to digest, not to mention that it is high in fat and calories. My suggestion: Adjust your dairy intake accordingly.

If you have trouble getting enough calcium in your diet, then try switching to enriched soy or rice milk. They taste just like 2 percent or nonfat milk, but they are better for you since they have zero fat. Just watch the label and make sure that they have been enriched with Vitamin D.

> *Most of us would benefit greatly from*
> *a calcium supplement.*
> *(See idea number 84.)*

Some people experience digestive problems associated with dairy, such as cheese. Cheese can literally clog your system. Sluggish digestion will make you feel heavy, tired, weak, and lethargic. These are not good feelings to have when trying to combat stress. In fact, it will make matters worse. Watch your diet and adjust your dairy intake according to your needs. You will feel better for it!

God has given us two incredible things:
absolutely awesome ability and freedom of choice.
The tragedy is that, for the most part,
many of us have refused them both.

FRANK DONNELLY

66
Drink Plenty of Water

WE KNOW we need to drink water, but we tend to forget how important it really is (75 percent of us are walking around dehydrated). Drink a ton of water every day! We are made up of water, and our bodies need water to survive. We can go weeks without food, but we can only go days without water. It is cleansing and healing.

The more stressed out you are, the more critical for you to drink enough water. Stress creates toxins, and the body uses water to eliminate those toxins through urination and sweating. Without proper hydration, those toxins remain in your body, and you can get sick.

If you exercise and work out, you need additional water. I tell my fitness classes to drink a full eight ounces before class as well as during class, and then they should drink another eight ounces after class. You know you are hydrating yourself correctly when you hit the bathroom on a regular basis. Are you drinking enough?

Coffee, sodas, and juice don't count. The caffeine in coffee and sodas actually dehydrates you. Soda and juices also have incredible amounts of sugar. Diet drink? It has chemicals that the body has to deal with, so it doesn't help the body at all. I love to have a diet soft drink every day because I love the flavor. But that makes it even more important for me to drink extra water to ensure my body can flush out any chemicals or toxins. If I don't drink enough water, I feel it. I keep large bottles of water in the refrigerator so I only have to grab one and go. I keep them refilled with cold, filtered water at all times.

If you still aren't convinced, here are a few more good reasons to drink water: Water reduces your chances of colon cancer and certain breast cancers, helps you eat less, increases brain power, and increases energy. Make it easy on yourself and your body. . .drink more water!

৵

If he is thirsty,
give him water to drink.

PROVERBS 25:21

67
Exercise

NOW I'M really pushing it, aren't I? I've suggested that you eat better, reduce your sweet intake, and now I'm bringing up exercise. You thought this was a stress management book not a health and fitness one, right? Well, it is! In order to manage our stress, though, we have to pay attention to our bodies. If we are truly going to live healthy, balanced lives then we must address each aspect of our lives: emotions, mind, body, and spirit. Exercise is paramount to our overall health.

The Aerobics and Fitness Association of America (AFAA) recommends that we engage in physical activity for at least thirty minutes a day at a minimum of 55 percent of our maximum heart rate (or level 5 or 6) three to five days a week (see idea number 61). Overall, Americans live sedentary lives, and we must get active. Most of us aren't farming and hunting anymore, so people's hearts don't get the workout that they did in years past. Therefore, we must exercise.

I mentioned earlier that people aren't exercising hard enough to receive any health benefit. What a shame! Make your workouts count by monitoring your FIT (frequency, intensity, and time). Exercise at least three days a week, but I would encourage you to do it five days a week. Our bodies were designed to move. The less we move, the greater the risk of illness. Make sure you are exerting yourself at the right level. Then, maintain that level of exercise for at least thirty minutes. If you can squeeze an hour in, better for you! We do not exercise for anyone but ourselves. You are worth it! We have to live with these bodies for a long time, so let's care for them.

❧

The body is a sacred garment.
It's your first and last garment;
it's what you enter life in
and what you depart life with, and
it should be treated with honor.

MARTHA GRAHAM

68
Jump Rope

I HAVE A dear friend who is in his "best chapter of life"—retirement. He is in excellent shape with lots of energy and good spirit. He's an inspiration to all who meet him. What's his secret? Jumping rope. Since his youth, he has been jumping rope every day without fail. Every day. . .did you catch that?

Most of us can remember jumping rope when we were young but say we haven't picked up a rope since then. I got into jumping rope some years ago while teaching my SportsCircuit class, and I love it. It is a great cardio workout and stress buster. Do you know what is even better about it? Short spurts of jumping rope, say ten minutes, give you the same effect or results as jogging for twenty minutes. I'm not kidding. Jumping rope pushes our heart rate into our target zone immediately and keeps it there for the duration. It is awesome!

I also like the fact that a jump rope is easy to travel with. I take one with me when I'm on the road in case my hotel does not have a fitness room. I can go outside in the parking lot and jump. Within ten minutes or so, I have gotten my cardio workout in. *Wham!* I'm done! Mind you, you will know you are working out. Jumping rope takes coordination, timing, and cardio capacity. If you are game to give it a try, start off slow. Time a minute and see if you can make it. Many people in my class couldn't endure one full minute their first time. But try again and again. Before you know it, you'll build your endurance and cardio capacity enough to sustain a decent workout.

Jumping rope shouldn't be labored or too intense. Done correctly, it is smooth. Watch any boxer, and you think they are floating. It isn't hard on the joints if you let the rope move with you. Stand tall and use the wrists to whip the rope around. You may even practice the motion first without the rope. Timing is everything, but you can do it.

I play music while I jump rope, and it provides an excellent outlet for stress. Try it! You can do it just about anywhere—except maybe not on the second floor when someone is sleeping on the bottom floor. Jump right in, and you might be another testimony later in life to its power.

Great men are they who see that the spiritual is
stronger than any material force,
that thoughts rule the world.

RALPH WALDO EMERSON

69
Build Strength

By NOW you understand the importance of exercising aerobically to keep your heart in good working condition. Taking aerobic classes or running will not keep you strong, though. In order to care for our muscles, we must strength train. You may dislike lifting weights. You may have had a bad experience or simply don't like the process, but let me share with you how critical it is for you to work your muscles.

Have you ever planted a new, tiny tree? In order for it to survive, you must stake it into the ground. Otherwise, the first wind would come along and blow it over. Its trunk just isn't strong enough to withstand the wind's force. If over time, however, you do not take the stakes off and allow the tree to grow thicker, it will remain thin and fragile. But if you take the stakes out after the tree has established its roots, it quickly learns that to sustain the resistance of the wind, it must grow a thicker trunk. Why do you think trees in the wilderness survive? They grow thick trunks!

Our bones are no different. If we simply move and exercise our heart, the muscles feel no need to strengthen or thicken. They will remain thin and frail. But, if you add resistance to your muscles (even light resistance), the muscles will pull on the bones, forcing them to become dense and strong. It's not just a matter of reducing stress by building stronger muscles; it is a matter of good health.

I certainly don't want to be hunched over with osteoporosis in my old age or break bones easily. One powerful way to prevent that is to weight train one to two times a week. Certainly, if you want to compete in a bodybuilding contest, you will need to work harder, but most of us simply want healthy bones and strength to endure life.

A good way to start is to purchase a couple of handheld weights. I suggest that women start with 5 to 8 pounds and men with 10 to 15 pounds. Remember, we aren't going for "buff" yet; we are simply adding resistance to our muscles.

Now, turn on some tunes you like and begin to swim. "Huh?" you exclaim. No, you don't need a pool. But, we are going to swim! Begin with the front stroke. Trust me, those light weights will soon feel heavier. Try to do at least twenty repetitions on each arm. Then, do the backstroke for the same count. Next, breaststroke and finish off with a dive, which involves lifting the weights above your head and pressing down along the sides of your body. This series alone works all of the arm muscles. Add some lunges and squats with weights, and you are on your way to a stronger, healthier you!

No one can defeat us
unless we first defeat ourselves.

Dwight D. Eisenhower

70
Stretch

DO YOU ever watch cats stretch? They can twist and turn their bodies into some amazing positions. They are not very active creatures, but they know the benefit of stretching. Unfortunately, we do not dedicate nearly enough time every week to stretching, and it can dramatically improve flexibility and reduce tension.

Just like exercise, the AFAA suggests that we stretch three to five days a week. Let me first define stretching. Real stretching is actively helping a muscle relax and elongate, especially after it has been exercised or contracted (tightened). We can stretch two ways:

1) Static—We hold the stretch and breathe through it, usually performed on the floor.

2) Limbering—We move the muscles at a slower pace, mirroring what we just exercised but with less intensity, concentrating on range of motion.

You may see people bounce when they stretch, which is called ballistic stretching. It is unsafe and, therefore, not recommended. The best kind of stretch for stress reduction is static.

What I like about static stretching is that it

requires focus and breathing through the stretch, which helps reduce our heart rate and blood pressure. We can also static stretch just about anywhere at anytime. If you sit in front of a computer all day, take breaks to stretch out your neck and shoulders. Physical therapists are now finding that carpel tunnel syndrome actually starts in the neck when we lean the head forward to look at the computer screen. Stretch your wrists and arms throughout the day, too.

Did you know that 80 percent of Americans suffer from back pain? Many times our backs need stretching and strengthening to be healthy. Make sure you are stretching your back several times a week, especially if you are active.

Combine stretching with some of the breathing exercises, and you have a great recipe for harmony. Who couldn't use a little more of that in his or her life?

No pessimist ever discovered the secrets to the stars,
or sailed to an uncharted land,
or opened a new heaven to the human spirit.

HELEN KELLER

71
Lie in the Grass

THE OLDER I get, the more I try to get in touch with my youth. I'm not trying to relive it—heavens no! But, I am trying to glean wisdom from that child in us that, unfortunately, can be lost through the journey to adulthood. Without knowing it, children cope with stress extremely well. I remember lying supine on the grass for hours and watching the clouds blow by. The clouds would begin to form into animals or familiar objects. Time, I felt, would stand still.

But we adults experience time flying by at warp speed! The treadmill we are on keeps going faster and faster, and we wonder how we will keep up. As soon as we realize that we can't and that we must push the pause button every now and then, we will be healthier and happier.

> *If you carry your childhood with you,*
> *you never become older.*
>
> ABRAHAM SUTZKEVER

Go to a park with a blanket. Don't bring a book or boom box. Don't plan to "do something" while you are there, and do not wear a watch. Simply lie on the grass and gaze heavenbound. Let yourself sink into the mood fully. Try some special breathing and relax. God is often in the gentle breeze. Give yourself permission to lose track of time, and see what happens. Often, special moments are the simplest moments.

Aches and pains are your body's way
of telling you something.
And have you ever noticed that
your body becomes more and more talkative
as you grow older?

ANONYMOUS

72
Sit in the Sun

SINCE WE are only given one body and we must make it last, I know the importance of caring for our skin. However, the sun is very healing and has elements our body needs to thrive. Research has shown that a little "sun therapy" reduces stress and tension. Sun can really brighten your day!

I try to sit outside in the sun a couple of times a week during my lunch break. I'm not there for long, maybe twenty minutes, but I let each ray kiss my skin. In twenty minutes, I can feel a hundred times better. Set aside some time and sit in the sun.

Use sunscreen and wear sunglasses to protect your eyes. And don't forget your lips and ears! Ouch. . .there's nothing like burned lips. You can use this time to practice other tips like praying, reading, or relaxing. You can eat a healthy lunch and really do your body some good. Just watch the time and don't lose track. Short periods are better for us, and we want you living a healthy, *long* life.

Sunshine, on my shoulder,

makes me happy.

JOHN DENVER

73
Ride a Bike

THE GROUP Queen had a silly song about riding a bike. Riding a bike *is* fun and can put a smile on your face. Do you remember those contraptions we used when we were younger? You know, they got us from point A to point B before we had a driver's license.

I had a purple bike with a yellow banana seat. And of course, I had tassels and a bell on the handlebar. I eventually upgraded to a blue ten-speed; and boy, that bike took me places. It also gave me a chance to be outside, away from the pressures of the world.

Our pressures have increased since childhood. They keep intensifying, so why not try mounting a bike and going for a spin? Check your tire pressure and make sure your brakes work. Then, head out for a nice ride in your neighborhood (don't forget your helmet). Bike riding is not only a great stress buster, but is a healthy activity for the entire family. Parents, kids, and dogs can all enjoy an evening ride.

I enjoy riding outdoors but also teach indoor cycling at a health club. It is a great option when the weather does not permit outdoor cycling. If you haven't ridden in awhile, take it easy your first time out. Realize your "seat" will be sore until you get used to the bike. Normally, it only takes a few classes to begin getting comfortable. Biking shorts also help alleviate the tenderness.

When riding, make sure your upper body is relaxed. When we are tense, we tend to tighten our shoulders, which restricts our breathing. Relax your hands and make sure you don't have a death grip. I try to change hand positions often to prevent the "white knuckle" syndrome. Keep your foot fairly flat, as it will lift on the rotation when it needs to. The most important aspect of cycling is to get your seat at the right height. Here's how:

Stand by your bike seat and lift the inner leg closest to the bike up to a 90-degree angle or where the top of your leg is flat enough to hold a book. The bike seat should be equal to or just slightly higher than the top of your leg. When you sit on the seat and have your foot flat on the pedal, you should have a soft curve behind your knee. If your knee is locked, the seat is too high, and you can hurt your knee. If you have too much curve behind your knee, the seat is too low, and you won't be able to push the pedals efficiently and will work harder than you need to.

Have the handlebars at such a height that your back is comfortable. Bring and drink plenty of water. Need a little boost of energy? Eat a banana before riding. They are an excellent, natural source of energy and potassium. Have fun and cycle away the blues.

If you do what you've always done,
you'll get what you've always gotten.

ANONYMOUS

74
Work in Your Garden

As I write this, it is spring. The flowers are in bloom. I have planted my vegetable garden, and a few seeds are sprouting. Gardening is so therapeutic. I love getting my hands in the soil, planting something new, and watching it grow. I enjoy weeding around the plant and pruning its dead limbs or flowers so it can thrive.

Gardening has so many correlations to our lives, too. I don't like yard work, though. The key word there is "work." My husband and I landscaped our entire yard for our first home: draining system, fences, patios, cement borders, plants, etc. It wasn't soothing or healing, it was just a ton of work! But a little gardening can definitely turn your gray skies blue.

If you don't have a little flowerbed, make one. Even if you hire out your yard maintenance, set aside a garden area as your special project. Get out once a week and tend to it. Use the time to reflect on your life and get some fresh air. Rake the soil and pull up any weeds. As you do so, think of your life. What is choking out your joy? What has overtaken your life and caused incredible stress? Pull it out!

Pick and prune the dead leaves and flowers off your plants. A plant can only concentrate on one thing at a time. If it has dead leaves, it will attempt to heal them rather than feeding the rest of the plant. Once you prune the dead leaves, the plant can put energy back into its healthy parts. What is dead in your life? What isn't supporting you or moving you toward a healthier life? If you don't pluck it, it will zap your energy.

Make sure you water your garden regularly. It cannot mature without water. Healthy gardens also need nutrients. Miracle Grow will get you immediate results, but is very surface oriented. Your plants will never push their root systems deep because they have been trained to receive all their nutrients from the surface. Ground fertilizer for plants, however, soaks in deep and forces the plant's root systems to move deep into the thick, rich soil.

Are you nourishing yourself properly and going deep? This book is a great start to guide you toward a healthier lifestyle, but you will want to go deeper. Make a commitment to care for yourself long term. Otherwise, you may just wilt and wither away.

*Puttering is
really a time to be alone,
to dream and to
get in touch with yourself.*

ALEXANDRA STODDARD

75
Go Camping

I RECENTLY attended a Renaissance Festival with a friend, and we were discussing living conditions that resembled camping or roughing it. My friend said, "My version of roughing it is a Motel 6," and I think many people feel the same way. I want to challenge you to explore the outdoors. God's wonderful earth offers us so much. I like to camp. In fact, I thought camping was putting everything you needed in a pack and hiking. My husband has since informed me that camping is pulling the car into a parking space and unloading the cooler full of goodies. In either case, try some of the great outdoors for a change of pace. It will do your body some good!

Now, I would like to offer some rules for camping. First of all, don't bring a portable television set or VCR. You have the galaxy to watch. Don't bring a boom box, but listen to nature's symphony. Leave the fancy clothes behind and be a slob for a couple of days. The wildlife won't care what you look like. In fact, the more you smell like the "city," the more bugs you will attract.

Do bring a hammock, a hat, sunscreen, bug repellent, and a good book. Take naps and long walks, and roast some marshmallows over an open fire. As you get in tune with nature, you will be amazed at how close to God you feel. The closer to His heart you become, the healthier you will become. And as you return home, take some of that health and peace back with you.

I have learned, in whatsoever state I am,
therewith to be content.

PHILIPPIANS 4:11 KJV

76
Go Fishing

OKAY, MAYBE I am strange. I not only enjoy camping, but I like to fish. I guess growing up in the Rocky Mountains influenced me. Fishing is a great escape for those who may not have the time or equipment to camp. You don't need to block out an entire weekend to fish, but it does require patience and demands that we slow down.

You can't rush fishing. The more you want to catch something, the longer it takes. Fish are smart. It is truly a game of intelligence. Although I am pleased when I catch something to eat, the process itself is tranquil—especially lake fishing. At a lake, you can pull up your lawn chair, cast out, and wait. As you let your hook sink a bit, you can gaze at the beautiful trees and rock formations around the lake. It is very calming for the nerves, unless you begin to take fishing too seriously.

There are voices which we hear in solitude,
but they grow faint and inaudible
as we enter into the world.

RALPH WALDO EMERSON

My favorite kind of fishing, though, is in a stream—when you have to walk and hike to just the right fishing hole. I imagine, if I were a fish, where would I hang out? Fishing a stream can also be more challenging. In either case, being outdoors and active transports us away from the hectic pace of ordinary life. For just a moment, we can be back in time, a time when watches and alarm clocks didn't dictate our day.

All you need is a fishing pole, some hooks, bait, and a license. Fishing is something the entire family can enjoy, or you can just be alone in the wilderness. Any time you can be outside, it is good for your body, mind, and soul—and that's not a fish story!

*A bad day fishing is better than
a good day anywhere else.*

ANONYMOUS

77
Join an Activities Club

TECHNOLOGY has driven us apart. The ads try to persuade us that we are more connected, but the truth is that we are isolating ourselves. Way back when, people would actually sit on their front porches and sip lemonade together. They weren't hurried but got lost in conversations and storytelling. Today, we don't know what a front porch looks like! We zoom in and out of our garages, never to interact with other people in our neighborhood. Our disconnection is spilling into all aspects of life. I suggest we plug back in!

Most community centers and churches have sports teams. Leagues have different levels of ability to accommodate almost anyone from the beginner to the hard-core sports star. Joining a league, getting to know others, and working as a team toward a common goal is rewarding and healthy. Joining a league is not only good for your body, but will also help your emotions because we were created for community.

Besides sports teams, most cities have hiking, biking, running, or climbing clubs. You aren't competing against another team or working together, but you are doing something you like together. Usually the club will have a set day and time to meet, and you set out on an adventure.

Live in a small town without many options? Organize something. I lived in a tiny town for awhile and started a beach volleyball outing every Saturday. I determined a day and time that I thought would work for most people. I then created a flyer and handed it out. I didn't know if I would have enough for two teams, but I did, and we met every Saturday from that day on. People would invite their friends, and the group grew. We had a blast playing in the sand and being together. No shop talk or worries were allowed on court. Get involved with something. Your body needs the outlet.

The race goes not always to the swift
but to those who keep on running.

Anonymous

78
Hire a Personal Trainer

WE USUALLY take care of our vehicles well. We regularly get them serviced to make sure they run properly. Yet, we do not always give the same care to our body. Most people call the doctor when they have a problem rather than taking preventive measures. We pay mechanics, and we see counselors, but we seldom hire a professional personal trainer to care for our body. But, our body needs the help.

Inside every person is a healthy body
just waiting to come out.

Although I am a certified personal trainer, I will work with another trainer every now and then to challenge my fitness level. To truly care for all of my body's needs, I need help, and so do you. A personal trainer will assess your fitness state—usually by measuring your body fat and aerobic capacity. We don't have to all look like models or weight lifters, but a personal trainer can help us get on the right path to having the best body possible. You will also learn a fitness program that will help you reach your personal goals. A word of caution: Many gyms hire out their personal trainers, and they may not be the best match for you. A professional personal trainer will listen to *your* needs and *your* goals and help you get there. Don't do anything that hurts or pushes you in the direction you don't want to go.

A personal trainer will also hold us accountable. If we are paying by the hour, we will perform. It's our nature. If we don't experience some financial pain, we don't take it as seriously. Make a commitment for three to six months to work with a trainer. You may think it costs a lot of money, but wouldn't you rather spend it on good health than on doctor visits and medications? Inside every person is a healthy body just waiting to emerge.

If you haven't got your health,
you haven't got anything.

ANONYMOUS

79
Sleep

SLEEP disorders are on the rise, and so is the use of sleeping aids. Sleep is paramount to our health.

Our muscles can repair simply by stopping whatever we are doing, but our minds must sleep in order to renew. I also believe our emotional health is as strong as the amount of sleep we receive. How many hours are you getting?

Everyone is different, but most research still indicates that we should get eight hours of sleep a night. Parents of newborn babies not only laugh at this statement, but also wonder if they'll ever sleep again. It's challenging, but do try to get more sleep.

Just like a battery, we need to be recharged. The busier we are, the more important it is for us to sleep. I can always tell when I'm not rested. Little things begin to bother me. Serving others becomes a burden rather than a joy. My attitude becomes a barometer and lets me know when I need additional sleep. How do you act when you don't get enough sleep?

The proper amount of sleep helps us fend off stress. When we have enough sleep, we can tackle the pressures of the day. When we are lacking, we get frustrated, discouraged, and overwhelmed. We get more stressed and can ultimately get sick. Even if it means hitting the hay earlier to get those eight hours, do it. Some people are really in tune with their bodies and know that they need more than eight hours of sleep. It is not a perfect world, but try to get a good, solid, restful night of sleep. New attitudes come with the morning.

❧

"Come to me,
all you who are weary and burdened,
and I will give you rest."

MATTHEW 11:28

80
Get a Massage

MY FIRST massage experience was not pleasant. I had just been in a car accident, and they were trying to "fix me." It was painful, but it did help. As a surprise during our honeymoon, my husband arranged for me to have a "real" massage. As I lay on the table motionless, my husband asked, "So, how was it?"

I could barely answer and couldn't move. I was a complete noodle. I thought I'd never walk again simply because I was so relaxed. I got hooked on the healing powers of a massage.

Our bodies work hard for us each day. They get us out of bed, walk us wherever we want, sit us down, pick us up, move things, type, process food, deal with chemicals, take in toxins. . .the list goes on. Massage is an awesome way to help our body process more efficiently. Massage gets the muscles relaxed and frees our bodies of knots we get from tension. Massage awakens certain aspects of the body and helps it move things through—that's why they encourage you to drink a lot of water after a massage. We can flush out all sorts of bad things after a massage.

A variety of massages exist: Swedish, reflexology, stone, and sports therapy. Take your pick. They each approach your massage a bit differently, but the idea is the same. . .to rid you of stress. Help your body do its job and get a massage at least a couple of times a month. Once again, it costs money, but it will be money well spent.

Burning your candles at both ends
only leads to burnout.

81
Hit a Spa

As I mentioned earlier, I am not a spa veteran, but I am working on it! My husband and I recently purchased a spa package in Mexico. We were not informed that our dates were during college spring break and, consequently, all of the students at the hotel overwhelmed us. The good news, however, was that the spa resort was empty. The bars were packed, but we had seclusion and superb customer service at the spa. Spas by their very existence are places to retreat. In fact, I came up with Stress Pushed Away for my little acronym. Are you overdue for some SPA action?

My favorite treatment is a pedicure. If you have not had someone give your feet attention for a full hour, you owe it to your feet to get a pedicure. They work hard each day supporting our entire body. Our feet get us from place to place without complaining, unless we wear the wrong shoes. Our feet need attention to remain healthy.

Manicures are also nice and keep your hands looking clean. Manicures can prevent dry skin, broken nails, or cracked skin. Any spa treatment is bound to soothe and relax you.

I have not experienced a mud treatment, but I know they are good for the skin. The dead skin is peeled away with the dry mud, leaving behind a soft layer of new skin, free of toxins.

Whatever interests you, visit a spa. Many of the larger facilities have swimming pools, mineral pools, hot tubs, saunas, and steam rooms that are free with the purchase of a spa treatment. Check it out! Remember: Stress Pushed Away!

If you don't take care of yourself,
no one else will.

ANONYMOUS

82
Burn Aromatherapy Candles

I LOVE THE look of any burning candle. The flickering light fills the room with warmth. Nothing creates atmosphere like candles. Aromatherapy candles not only look comforting, but they also smell heavenly.

If you have a stressful job, you might consider burning a candle at work. You don't want something that will make you sleepy like chamomile, but lavender would be nice and calming.

Burn some candles at home, too. Our sense of smell is amazing. By smelling something soothing, we can trick our mind and emotions into thinking we aren't stressed. Cinnamon or vanilla is wonderful for that "home-baked pie" touch. Consider an aromatherapy candle your own SPA treatment at a fraction of the cost. Light 'em up and burn them!

❧

To be simple is to be great.

RALPH WALDO EMERSON

83
Maintain Good Body Posture

I ALREADY shared with you the importance of building muscle strength to support healthy bones, but your body posture is just as important.

If you spend your days hunched over with your shoulders drooping, you create a negative state for yourself. How can your mind and emotions be positive when your body is in a negative position? A quick way to pick up your mood is to simply sit up straight.

Sitting up straight and standing tall also allow your body to breathe properly. When we open up our chest and press the shoulders back and down, we give our lungs and heart more room to work. Therefore, they can be more effective. The more oxygen your body receives, the better it can process stress. Good posture takes effort, though.

If you are not used to standing up straight, your back muscles may not be strong enough to maintain good posture. Here's a great trick to help: Put a tennis ball under each armpit and place your arms by your side. To keep the tennis balls from slipping, you must squeeze your arms in, which lowers your shoulders into proper alignment. Walk around the house for ten minutes and see how you feel. Extend the time as you build the endurance.

Practice good posture wherever you are, and you will breathe better and feel stronger. Remember, your mind and emotions look to your body for a cue. If you are standing with confidence, your mind and body will support you with courageous thoughts and feelings! Go, beat stress, win!

Be proud and stand tall.

84
Take Vitamins

ALTHOUGH I am not a nutritionist, I can tell you aren't getting enough vitamins and minerals in your diet. None of us can get what our bodies need anymore. Unfortunately, even fruits and vegetables are not as nutritional as they once were. Everything is being picked earlier so it can be shipped farther, resulting in weaker food. Most fruits and vegetables gain their highest power when they ripen. The riper the fruit is, the better it is for consumption. But, ripe foods spoil quickly; thus, the dilemma. A viable solution is to take supplements.

I highly recommend that you only take gel capsules. The hard-pressed vitamins are difficult for the body to digest. In fact, most of us pass them through without receiving any benefit. The gel caps, on the other hand, are quickly absorbed into our system. If you are going to spend the money, at least get something your body can use.

Every one of us should take a multivitamin. I like the ones that are designed specifically for gender and life stages because they add certain minerals that aid each sex and age. Vitamin C is a great antioxidant and immune booster. And calcium is vital, especially for women, because it helps build stronger bones.

If you are confused, talk to your doctor or a nutritionist about what is best for you. Some supplements can react with certain medications, so get clearance first if you are taking medications.

Supplements can give your body a boost and help it combat stress—creating a great, healthy life for you!

⁊

What we love,
we shall grow to resemble.

BERNARD OF CLAIRVAUX

85
Take the Stairs

THE STAIRS are an exceptional way to burn stress and calories. I spent twenty years of my life in Colorado and lived by a set of stairs that went straight up the face of a mountain. I would run up the nearly three hundred steps to the top and stumble my way down. I got smart one day and decided to power walk the stairs instead. Wow! What a workout. I was able to repeat the steps three times and got more of a burn in my legs because I was going at a slower pace. Steps are everywhere; take advantage of them.

At the office, especially when you are under pressure, take the stairs instead of the elevator. I know some executives who change clothes during their lunch hour and "climb the stairs" as their workout. It's convenient and quick. Locate a beach with narrow steps winding down to the coast and walk down, walk around, and then climb back up the stairs. You are combining a peaceful experience with a little exercise. Multitasking at its best!

To achieve anything, we must take the first step. Step up!

Men will get no more out of life
than they put into it.

WILLIAM J. H. BOETCKER

SECTION IV

RECONNECTING WITH OUR MAKER

86
Pray

PRAYER IS a powerful tool for beating stress. Unfortunately, many people use it as a last resort rather than the first step to settle their harried spirit. I think the following poem sums it up nicely:

I got up early one morning
and rushed right into the day.
I had so much to accomplish
that I didn't have time to pray.

Problems just tumbled about me,
and heavier came each task.
"Why doesn't God help me?"
I wondered. He answered,
"You didn't ask."

I wanted to see joy and beauty.
But the day toiled on gray and bleak;
I wondered why God didn't show me.
He said, "But you didn't seek."

I tried to come into God's presence;
I tried every key in the lock.

God gently and lovingly chided,
"My child, you didn't knock."

I woke up early this morning,
and paused before starting my day.
I had so much to accomplish
that I had to take time to pray.

ANONYMOUS

Prayer is a form of communicating with God. Besides feeling connected and loved, through prayer, you will also realize you aren't alone. Many times, stress makes us feel isolated, like we are the only ones on the planet suffering. Don't fall into the trap. Pray! And don't forget that you can pray anytime, anywhere.

Prayer may not change my circumstances,
but it will change me.

C. S. LEWIS

87
Meditate

HAVE YOU ever noticed how noisy our world has become? We are bombarded with advertising in more places and ways than ever before, and technology invades every aspect of our life. Society trains us from a very young age to rush and be productive *all* of the time. Slowing down to reflect and meditate is definitely going against the stream, but that is a good thing. Those in the stream are drowning from an overload of stress! Don't join them. Swim against the tide.

Meditation can be an intimidating concept when we believe it is only for the professional minister. But anyone (and everyone) should meditate. What exactly is meditation? It is simply reflecting and pondering. That sounds easy enough. But in order to meditate, you must first be quiet. Shhhh. . .

Learn to get in touch with
the silence within yourself
and know that everything in this life
has a purpose.

ELISABETH KUBLER-ROSS

Today more than ever before, it is difficult to quiet our minds. We have schedules, tasks, commitments, activities, and a myriad of other "things" that fill our mind and clog it. We must flush these things out before we can freely reflect on the higher things of life. A great way to let go is to journal. In order to make a connection with God and strengthen that relationship, you must be still and listen.

Breathing exercises can help you meditate. Try sitting on the floor with your legs crossed. Let your arms hang on your side and rest on your thighs. Tilt your head upward as you breathe in and hold it for twenty seconds. As you release your breath over fifteen seconds, lower your head. Stack yourself back up with your head forward and repeat. Each time, you are quieting your spirit and preparing yourself to listen to God.

Make time each day to just "be" and let your spirit connect with God. Reflect on the riches of life—and I don't mean money or material possessions. Clear your mind of the clutter and see what God gives you. You can trust that it won't be more stress!

May my meditation be pleasing to him,
as I rejoice in the LORD.

Psalm 104:34

88
Be Grateful

YOU'VE HEARD the saying "A grateful heart is a happy heart," right? I think that saying has been around so long because it is true. Unfortunately, the pressures of life can turn us into whiners. We seem to focus more on what isn't working. Even if things do go well, we often complain about the timing. Nothing seems to be good enough. With such impossible standards, we create huge amounts of stress for ourselves.

Anyone who has traveled to a third-world country understands how blessed we are in the United States. We have it all, but many don't even know it. Many years ago, a Russian exchange student stayed with me. I was single and lived in a great two-bedroom condo with vaulted ceilings, an oversized living room, and a cozy fireplace. I'll never forget the Russian girl's expression as she saw the size of my apartment. When she walked in, she asked, "How many families live here with you?"

I was embarrassed to answer, "Only me." She toured my place in sheer amazement. She then told me that in her country, three to four families would share the space of my living room alone. I was humbled.

Don't forget for a single second how good you have it. Our greatest challenge in this country isn't dealing with tangible, material scarcity but overcoming our spiritual poverty!

You may not have as many toys as your neighbor, but so what? Be grateful for what you *do* have and stop trying to keep up with the Jones family. They are stressed out trying to keep up with the Johnsons. Be grateful. You really are blessed.

Thank God every morning when you get up
that you have something to do,
which must be done,
whether you like it or not.

CHARLES KINGSLEY

89
Marvel at His Majesty

RONALD REAGAN once said, "Double—no triple—our troubles and we'd still be better off than any other people on earth." We have it good! Our country is incredibly beautiful and offers so much. When was the last time you took a good look and absorbed God's creation to its fullest?

Every plant, tree, flower, bird, insect, and animal is from God. Each has its purpose and place. As humans, we get to enjoy everything to its fullest. Too often, though, we are in such a hurry that we zoom by and miss opportunities.

Sights, sounds, and smells can soothe your soul and ease your mind. My husband and I ride motorcycles with friends. We all love getting on the open road. We've often described it as being a part of life rather than sitting and watching it. When you are in a car, it is like watching a movie. You can see everything, but it is at a distance. When you are on a motorcycle, every part of nature is nearer to you. Now I'm not suggesting you run out and get your license, but I am advocating that you stop to smell the roses and pause to ponder this magnificent world we live in. If you don't feel awe when you marvel at

His majesty, then you aren't really living. Wake up
and be healed.

America's beauty is not only in its features;
its beauty is in the character
underneath those features.

LUCI SWINDOLL

90
Trust God

HAVE YOU ever noticed that the older we get, the more difficult it is for us to trust people? People repeatedly let us down, and we get hurt. Before they know it, some people won't trust anyone. But this is a lonely place to live. If we don't let ourselves count on anyone, then we carry the load of life alone. We may not get hurt, but we won't get connected or grow, either.

I have learned that people are human and will therefore disappoint us. The good news, however, is that we can count on one Person 24/7. . .God.

God never intended for us to go it alone. He created us for a relationship with Himself and with others. He made each of us, and we can trust that He has our best interests at heart.

You may have a difficult time believing this right now. Perhaps you are in a terrible situation and wonder where God is. God hasn't gone anywhere. He is the one who will get you through if you only let Him. When my mother was dying and I was going through a nasty divorce, I remember telling God, "I know you don't give more than a person can handle, but I think you have me mixed up with someone else!"

I was stressed out beyond description, and my health showed it. My weight dropped to 97 pounds, even though I was nearly 5' 10". Through reflection and meditation, I was reminded that these things happen because the world is not perfect. People make decisions that negatively impact others, and illness just happens. But no matter what, I could count on God's love. He was my strength.

How about you? What do you face? Nothing is too big or too small for God. The only thing you have to lose by trusting Him is your stress.

Trust and believe!

91
Live What You Believe

HOW MANY times have you heard "Walk your talk"? This saying reminds us that if we expect others to believe what we say, we must live consistent lives. Someone once said, "People don't care how much you know until they know how much you care." How true! How much do you trust someone you don't know? Without connection, rapport, and trust, a person doesn't have much leverage with you. But once you establish a relationship and begin to build trust, you are more open to what they have to say. So we must live whatever we believe. If we don't, we live a lie and create strife in our own lives.

Many people don't really know what they believe, so they can't live it. Too often, people adopt the beliefs of their family or friends. But you must know what *you* stand for so securely that if you were confronted with the opposite, you would stand your ground.

Get to the root of your beliefs. Explore them and own them! Then you can begin living those beliefs with confidence and drawing others closer to you. Living what you believe is a quick way to create inner peace. Don't delay.

*You came into this world crying
and everyone around you was smiling.
Live your life in such a way that in the end,
you are smiling,
and everyone around you is crying at the loss.*

ANONYMOUS

92
Forgive Yourself

MANY OF us are good at forgiving others. We have learned that, in life, people will hurt us. In order to prevent tension, we must forgive.

However, I think many people are harder on themselves than on others, and they are failing to forgive themselves. This prevents us from having peace and from having a loving relationship with our Maker.

I have certainly made decisions and mistakes that I'd rather forget. We are all products of our pasts, which include our mistakes. By remembering what we did wrong in our past, we can make better choices today. Isn't that what life is about? Learning from our past? What is not acceptable is for us to beat ourselves up. Being hard on yourself will not correct your past or erase it. In fact, the more energy you give to beating yourself up, the more alive the mistake stays. Our Maker did not intend for you to have such guilt. God offers His forgiveness to us all. Doesn't it make sense for us to extend the same forgiveness to ourselves? Be kind to yourself.

How unhappy is he who cannot forgive himself.

PUBLIUS SYRIUS

What are you holding onto? If you cling to something from your childhood, remind yourself that you didn't have the tools you do today. As an adult, you may have made different decisions. But you didn't. Accept responsibility and move on! You made a mistake. Learn from it and share it with others so they won't make the same mistake. When we can help others, we truly heal ourselves.

Remember, forgiveness is a gift from God. Don't deny it. Embrace it and feel its power in your life.

❧

Forgiveness is not an elective
in the curriculum of life.
It is a required course,
and the exams are always tough to pass.

CHARLES SWINDOLL

93
Read the Word

DO YOU know why some books are called best-sellers? Because they have sold more copies than most books sell. In order to sell that many copies, a book must have a message that people want to read. Such a book exists that has life principles, guiding messages, hope, encouragement, and love: It is the Bible. Have you read it lately? It is the first book published on stress management, and it *will* change your life.

Some people see reading the Bible as an over-whelming chore. With the right Bible and attitude, however, it is an adventure. Try a study Bible that has everything broken down to daily passages, combined with stories and insights to help bring the points to a personal level. One of the most "real" versions is *The Message*. It is written in current language, which helps readers understand the principles.

Whatever version you have, read it. I was given advice once that really changed my heart. A pastor said, "If we were supposed to have all the answers, they would be in the book." Don't get hung up on questions like "Did God create the world in seven days or was it longer?" Who really cares how long it took Him? The bottom line is that God created us and the world in a wonderful way. Focus on the hope, encouragement, and love that are woven throughout every page.

Besides inspiring you, the Bible will keep you connected to God. The closer you are to Him, the more peace you will experience. God never changes. When people ask, "Where is God?" they are the ones who have moved far away, not Him. Get close. Read about Him and discover what He can do for your life. Be prepared for a change!

Your word is a lamp to my feet
and a light for my path.

PSALM 119:105

94
Attend a Healthy Church

I ACCEPTED Christ into my life at the age of thirteen, when my earthly father passed away. I began attending church to learn more about my heavenly Father and to build a strong relationship with Him.

Church hasn't always been a pleasant experience for me. Some churches are very legalistic, concentrating on rules rather than on love. Other churches are hypocritical, saying one thing but doing another. Are all churches bad? No. But, all churches are made up of people—people just like you and me. I have been told painful, hurtful things by people who attend church that those outside church walls would never say.

The lesson isn't to give up on church but to put it in its place. The church is just an instrument of God, not a god. It is a place for people to gather and worship together, not *be* worshipped. Keep your eyes upward, and you'll get what you need.

Looking for a church to attend isn't an easy task. We often have high expectations: child care, music, small groups, recreational activities, youth group, strong pastor, excellent messages, etc. Certainly, we want to be a part of something that meets our needs, but I challenge you to focus less on what a church is doing and concentrate more on its health. Are the members faithful? Does the church have long-standing members? Has the staff been on board for some time?

Don't merely look at the surface, but dig deeper. Discover what the church believes and compare that to your core values. If you have a match, other things will fall into place. In fact, if a church is missing something you would like to see, volunteer to make it happen.

When should you attend church? As one pastor says, "In town? In church!" God always has something to say if we are willing to listen. Find a place that works for you, and get connected to His love and purpose for your life. Remember, it is difficult to keep negative stuff in when you are filling yourself with the positive. Fill 'er up!

Anybody can observe the Sabbath
but making it holy surely takes the rest of the week.

ALICE WALKER

95
Join a Small Group

CHURCHES come in all sizes, but many are growing, making it difficult for those of us who attend them to get to know each other better. Our church has two services on Saturday night and four on Sunday morning. It is nearly impossible to meet everyone and connect on a deeper level. However, our church encourages every member to participate in small groups. Small groups are gatherings where people can get real with each other.

Everyone needs help from everyone.

BERTOLT BRECHT

One thing many people do not like about church is the appearance of "all is well." Too many people erroneously think that while at church, they should pretend that everything in their lives is fine. The church should be *the* place we go to for support, but it is often the last place we try. The only way to change this is by one person at a time, taking the chance to "get real."

Join a small group that fits your personality and

interests. Small groups exist to provide a social outlet, connect you to people, and help you manage
life's pressures. God created us for relationships, and
relationships provide security, hope, help, and love
for us. We could all use more real friends—and could
be a real friend. Get connected. Your heart and soul
will be happier.

A man is called selfish
not for pursuing his own good,
but for neglecting his neighbor's.

RICHARD WHATELY

96
Find the Good in All Circumstances

WE ARE spiritual beings by design. This separates us from animals. When we are young, I believe we are better in touch with our spirit or intuition. We don't question it, but simply listen to it. As we get older, though, we try to ignore it. If we let our spirit burn out, we will live an unhappy, unfulfilled life. One way to ensure that you keep your spark alive is to find the good in all circumstances of life.

"All circumstances?" you ask. Yes. Not all the situations we face are good—some are very bad—but in my life, positive things resulted from the bad. I became a better person. I am more whole, mature, and spiritual because of hardships I've faced. You have the same opportunity, but it takes effort. You must decide how you will handle painful situations before they occur. Because once the heat is on, you will not have time to think. You must react and focus on the positive.

He who seeks trouble will always find it.

ENGLISH PROVERB

I know some clouds appear to have no silver lining. Recently, a friend of mine lost her fifty-two-year-old husband. He was healthy and active, but leukemia attacked with a vengeance. What makes this more tragic is that my friend had endured two abusive marriages before finding this loving husband. It doesn't make sense, and it hurts. We will trust, though, that God will bring something good out of it. Already, people from all stages of his life are coming forward in support. My friend has asked them to take the time to appreciate those close to them and to thank those people who have made a difference. If some people live a more loving, compassionate life as a result of this, then something good did result from a horrible event. You, too, will see good things come from your life struggles. Keep looking for it, and you will find it.

But if, on the other hand, you continue to expect bad things and focus on the pain, that is what you will see. Bad things happen in life, but God will be there for you. You may need to hang on through the storm, but the morning will come. Look for the positive in life. Good is out there.

People only see what they are prepared to see.

RALPH WALDO EMERSON

97
Read an Inspirational Poem

I HAVE BEEN writing poetry since I was a child. Many people have written inspiring messages on paper for the world to enjoy. Regardless of the author's background, lifestyle, or faith, I believe poetry is of the heart and soul, which makes it a wonderful way to stay spiritually connected.

Pick up a poetry book and read. Let the words fill your spirit. Feel the warmth, love, and hope. Poetry books also make a great daily devotional guide. You can read a poem, reflect upon it, meditate, and pray.

Contrary to popular opinion, poetry isn't for wimps but for those strong enough to get in touch with their spiritual side and connect with God. Are you strong enough to learn from poetry?

The only thing that stands between
a man and what he wants from life
is often merely the will to try it
and the faith to believe that it is possible.

RICHARD M. DEVOS

98
Write God a Love Letter

WHEN WAS the last time you had a heart-to-heart talk with God? I mean the kind of communication where you are brutally honest? Are you afraid to be completely open? God is big enough to handle anything you bring Him. In fact, He already knows everything about you, even the number of hairs on your head! But the communication process is for *our* benefit.

I find that writing letters to God is a good way to communicate my thoughts. Even in our high-tech society, handwritten notes and letters have more impact. Our handwriting is personal and can come straight from our soul. Write God a love letter. Share with Him your frustrations, disappointments, heartaches, and questions.

"Wait," you say. "I thought this was supposed to be a love letter?" It is, but it is a *real* love letter. It is the kind that bears all because during the process of releasing the negative things, all that will remain is love.

God is waiting for you to turn your pain over to Him. He wants you to sense His love, be loved, and give love. Writing it out might just be the ticket for your freedom. Try it!

Your letter need not be formal or follow any formula. Simply speak to God through your pen and paper. If you find yourself praising and thanking Him, that is awesome. But don't pretend you don't have any issues. We all have "stuff" that bothers us; what we do with it is what sets us apart.

Once you have written your letter and turned it over to God, you might want to burn it. As you watch the paper burst into flames, let it signify the destruction of those negative issues in your life. Let love replace the spaces it leaves behind—God has plenty to give.

The amazing thing about love is that it is the best way to get to know ourselves.

ROLLO MAY

99
Get Involved

HAVE YOU ever been too busy to help others or get involved at church or local programs? If so, you are missing out, and you aren't as spiritually connected as you could be. We were created to give to one another.

Each one of us has special talents that become useless if we don't apply them. Your gifts weren't given to you for you to hoard or protect. No, they were given to you to share. The more in tune we are with others' needs, the closer to God we become. Helping people is what He is all about.

> *Don't be so heavenly minded*
> *you are of no earthly good.*
> *Don't be so earthly minded that*
> *you are of no heavenly good.*
>
> ANONYMOUS

I like to contribute both to my church and the community. I volunteer to help where I feel I am a fit. Currently, I am teaching a SportsCircuit class at church to help people get healthy. I am also facilitating business lunch programs to assist small businesses with their challenges. I'm giving back. What are you doing?

I know your schedule is already full, but if you apply idea number 33, you should have some extra time for serving others. What kind of life do we have if we don't have time for others? I suspect it is one of stress and strain, not one of pleasures and peace.

I'll give you something else to seriously consider that may encourage you to get involved. If you were to find yourself in great need today, who would support you? If you aren't investing in anyone else's life, do you think others will respond to your needs? Perhaps, but perhaps not.

We need each other to take action and get involved. When you do this, besides being personally blessed, you will feel more connected to your spiritual purpose. Remember, stress comes from being out of alignment. Realign yourself and do something to help out! When we each play our part, we all win.

The deeds you do may be the only sermon
some persons will hear today.

SAINT FRANCIS OF ASSISI

100
Worship

MANY PEOPLE associate worship with a certain music style. We can sing praises through other ways than singing hymns or worship songs, though. We can use all sorts of genres of music to lift our eyes toward the heavens with hearts of thanksgiving. I love a group called "The Dancing Saints." This techno/dance group takes traditional tunes and gives them some attitude. When I listen, I am connected with God. Worship is important for our relationship with God. What are you doing to stay connected?

Did you know that you can worship God in many ways, not just through music? Your life can reflect God's love. Every positive choice you make is worship; every kind deed you perform is worship; and every caring word you say is worship. Let your expressions, actions, and words show those around you that you are tapped into the Source.

Plug in to God and worship Him with your emotions, mind, body, and soul. Your life will be better for it, and you just might make a difference in others' lives.

101
Let Go and Let God

THROUGHOUT this book, I have provided tips, ideas, and suggestions, hoping to encourage you to manage your life and stress better so you can live a healthier, happier life. I hope your life will be touched and changed forever. But, everything in this book is a moot point if idea number 101 is not applied: You must let go and let God.

You may think you have control over your life, but just ask someone who is battling cancer to find out how "out of control" a person really is. Or ever have an ailment that doctors cannot diagnose or treat? At these times in life, we begin to comprehend how very small and incapable we are in the scheme of things and how very BIG and powerful God is. What is impossible for man is possible with God. Do you believe that?

Stress is a fact of life. It is associated with good and bad circumstances. How we manage stress is the key to healthy living. If we continually try to just cope with stress, we are like the rat on the wheel. We will go round and round, never getting anywhere until, one day, we fall off and drop dead. You must have that higher purpose and power to truly defeat negative stress—then you can survive and thrive amid life's curveballs. Give up what torments you. Hand it over to God. He's tough.

A better life awaits you—one with balance, harmony, peace, and love. By reading this book, you have made a great step toward that new life. Commit to applying several of these ideas. Share your excitement with others. You *can* attain healthier, happier living. Go for it. God is with you on your journey, and I'm also rooting for you!

Trust in the LORD with all your heart
and lean not on your own understanding.

PROVERBS 3:5–6

Conclusion

GOOD JOB! You have made first steps toward a healthier you by reading this book. But now it's your turn to take the next steps.

One reason we don't attain our goals is
that we often focus
on how far away we are from feeling satisfaction
rather than how far we've come.

FRED PRYOR

Reading this book was an action step, but you must now apply the principles to your life by making better choices each day and weighing the costs associated with every decision. If you want a different life, then you must do things differently. Do the same things you have always done, and you will end up at the same place you have always ended up—unfulfilled, unhappy, or maybe even worse. The ultimate cost of living a chaotic, stressful life is an early death. Do you want to pay that price?

My husband and I were in Seattle attending a conference on how to be better coaches. The president of the company was telling us about the latest trends and began to badger the audience about not working hard enough. He said if we weren't rich, it was because we weren't working around the clock. He was proud that he had no time for a life or relationships. He certainly was a successful man. He started his company as a one-man show and built it into an empire. He was speaking around the world and making really good money. Three months after we saw him at the conference, we learned that he had died of a massive heart attack—at the age of forty-four. He paid the ultimate price for not balancing his life. Are you at risk?

I saved sharing my testimony about stress until the end. I have given you bits and pieces of my story, but I now want you to know that stress just about beat me back in 1997. Until then, I had minimal stress management skills. With working eighty hours a week, I didn't have any balance, either. At the time, I thought I did a superb job of balancing work, home, friends, family, and personal interests. And I did do everything I was "supposed to do." I never missed a birthday party, employee anniversary celebration, or important meeting. I faithfully attended church and fitness classes. I kept the house, yard, and cars immaculate. I cooked from scratch. . .every night.

I appeared to have it all together, but I wasn't caring for myself. My life was organized, but *I* was out of control. I failed to manage my own emotional stress. I internalized everything and didn't have the right equipment to combat stress, so it was eating me from the inside out.

Everything came to a crashing head in the winter of 1996, when I was dealing with a horrible divorce and my mother's terminal illness. My body no longer let me ignore it. By the spring of 1997, I dropped down to 97 pounds at 5' 10". I stopped eating and nearly lost my will to live. Stress was winning.

I didn't know what to do, but I knew I couldn't keep living like this. Then one evening around 8:00 P.M., I had a vision. God presented a movie to me. He played it right there in front of me, as clear as day. I was in it. I was walking down a dirt road. I was tired, hungry, and lugging a massive black suitcase. I could barely move it, and I was crying as I used both arms to try to move it. I'd take a couple of steps and then would drop the suitcase. It was just too heavy. I began to sob. I fell to the ground and wailed, "I can't go on. I can't do this anymore." My head was in my hands.

Just then, I saw two dusty feet in sandals standing by me. I looked at them and could tell they had walked a lot of miles. As I lifted my head, I saw the worn-out robe tied with a rope. I found myself looking into Jesus' eyes. His eyes soothed me. Without a word, He pulled me off of the ground. He wrapped His arm around me and pulled me close. My weeping grew deeper, straight from my soul.

We began to walk together, but I remembered

my bag was still on the ground. I reached for my stuff, but He said, "No." He shook His head and drew me closer to His heart. "You are what matters to me, not your material possessions or what you do," poured into my heart from His. We began walking again. My tears started to subside, and I regained strength. I've never been the same. My prayer is that the actions you take will forever change your life. Don't wait until it is too late.

Life is a special gift from God. None of us is guaranteed smooth sailing or a set amount of time. But you can count on God to be there for you, loving and supporting you all the way. I learned a valuable lesson: Balance and a healthier, happier life are more than juggling tasks; it is about taking care of what truly matters—yourself.

I had to relearn what I needed to relax. I had to discover ways to de-stress that worked for me. I had to find outlets for my internal struggles. And I'm pleased to report that today I'm just as productive as I used to be, but I care for my needs now. I enjoy movies, hot baths, meditation, and prayer. I get plenty of sleep, eat right, and have fun. I'm living a healthier, happier life.

Plenty of things come our way that we have absolutely no control over, but we can choose to manage our stress better. Make the most of every day and manage it well. Your life is worth small changes today in order to prevent massive issues in the future.

Decide now to live a healthier, happier life. Fill in your success contract at the front of this book with ideas that you are willing to apply immediately. Take some action now and get going! Beat stress and win. Live a full and happy life. You deserve it!

Don't forget until it's too late that
the business of life
is not business, but living.

B. C. FORBES

BIBLIOGRAPHY

Ban Breathnach, Sarah. *Simple Abundance: A Daybook of Comfort and Joy.* New York, NY: Warner Books, a Time Warner Company, 1995.

Buzzell, Dr. Sid (General Editor). *The Leadership Bible* (New International Translation). Grand Rapids, MI: The Zondervan Corporation, 1998.

Cook, John. *The Book of Positive Quotations.* Minneapolis, MN: Rubicon Press, Inc., 1993.

Gallwey, W. Timothy. *The Inner Game of Tennis.* New York, NY: Random House, 1997.

Van Ekern, Glenn. *Speaker's Sourcebook II.* Englewood Cliffs, NJ: Prentice Hall, Inc., 1994.

ABOUT THE AUTHOR

LORRAINE Bossé-Smith is a personal trainer, fitness instructor, consultant, and life coach who lives in California with her husband, Steve, and cat, Wuz. She helps people across the country enhance their personal and professional relationships, increase their productivity, and improve the quality of their lives. If you need assistance in getting your life back on track and focusing on your priorities, contact Lorraine at www.thetotalyou.biz.

Lorraine is also the author of *Staying Fit with Style*, which is scheduled to release in fall 2004.

Inspirational Library

Beautiful purse/pocket-size editions of Christian classics bound in flexible leatherette. These books make thoughtful gifts for everyone on your list, including yourself!

When I'm on My Knees The highly popular collection of devotional thoughts on prayer, especially for women.
Flexible Leatherette. $4.97

The Bible Promise Book Over 1,000 promises from God's Word arranged by topic. What does God promise about matters like: Anger, Illness, Jealousy, Love, Money, Old Age, and Mercy? Find out in this book!
Flexible Leatherette. $3.97

Daily Wisdom for Women A daily devotional for women seeking biblical wisdom to apply to their lives. Scripture taken from the New American Standard Version of the Bible.
Flexible Leatherette. $4.97

A Gentle Spirit With an emphasis on personal spiritual development, this daily devotional for women draws from the best writings of Christian female authors.
Flexible Leatherette. $4.97

Available wherever books are sold.
Or order from:

Barbour Publishing, Inc.
P.O. Box 719
Uhrichsville, OH 44683
www.barbourbooks.com

If you order by mail, add $2.00 to your order for shipping.
Prices are subject to change without notice.